Beyond the Bars

Writing What You Couldn't Say

R. Suzanne Zeitman, Tamara Graham,
Ann Holdreith, John Morris, Joyce Harlukowicz,
Patricia Washburn, Dale Prentiss,
Rhonda Hacker, Linda Dominik,
Maureen Dunphy, Jim Perkinson

Edited by Margo LaGattuta

Plain View Press
P O 33311
Austin, TX 78764
1-800-878-3605
plainviewpress.com
SBRIGHT1@austin.rr.com

Cover art:

"Metamorphosis VI" is a Japanese woodblock print by Yoriko Hirose Cronin.

My current work comes from the fundamental theme of opposites as it exists in nature and the human experience in modern day Japan. Telephone poles, antennas, boats and the trees are metaphors of an irresistible resilience the Japanese people display in their obstructive and chaotic society.

The Japanese people can't completely escape their traditional customs and manners. I now find myself embracing their customs in the Western world that has been my home for the past thirty years.
Yoriko Cronin

Photographs:

Photographs of writers courtesy of Rick Smith, Rick's Photography, 333 Main Street, Rochester, Michigan.

Acknowledgments:

The editor wishes to acknowledge prior publication of the following piece: "Up an Unfamiliar Trail," *Everywhere is Someplace Else*, Plain View Press, © 1998 Margo LaGattuta.

Perhaps the truth lies
beyond the lines . . .

Contents

Margo LaGattuta

Foreword

I've always believed the best catalysts for writing are the ideas, thoughts and feelings I don't understand yet. Writing takes me on an exploration of the mysteries in the world and in myself, and when the creative process works, on a mission to try to name the unnamable. That makes writing exciting—and also dangerous—but I'm compelled to do it. Those feelings that gather in my heart and cannot be expressed imprison me. I look for words to wrap around the diaphanous smoke of thought and feeling that clouds me in, and often the essence of what I want to say is just beyond the lines. Hopefully, you, the reader, also bring meaning to my images. Your memories and life experiences enter my words like soaring blackbirds and, in the infinite sky of ideas, we meet.

Beyond the Lines is a collection of the poems, stories and essays of eleven writers who worked together in a group with me for over a year to bring their truths into language. Selected for their strong writing and editing skills, the writers represent many careers: teacher, minister, letter carrier, editor, training coordinator, actress, and consultant. It was a gift to be part of this collaboration and to watch a wide range of voices find common ground and meaning. Thank you to Suzanne, Tamara, Ann, John, Joyce, Patricia, Dale, Rhonda, Linda, Maureen and Jim for the many dynamic Sundays we've spent together birthing this project. Collectively, we decided on the subtitle, *Writing What You Couldn't Say*, because of our dedication to the power of making art with words. This book has become the celebration of a process that can open up meaning for everyone.

Beyond the Lines is the fifth Michigan anthology in a national literary series called New Voices from Plain View Press in Austin, Texas. We want to thank publisher Susan Bright for her creative input and for having the insight to encourage collaborative writing communities across the country to bring strong contemporary works into plain view. Her unique press is preserving the voices of quality writers and artists from every walk of life who should be heard.

We also thank Alan Cary, of Cary Gallery in Rochester, Michigan, for giving us a private showing of artwork in his gallery. Through him we discovered the dynamic woodcut, "Metamorphosis VI," by Yoriko Hirose Cronin, that graces our cover.

Here is a poem of my own that speaks to our theme of entering the world of mystery with language.

Up an Unfamiliar Trail

I see tiny hairs on the back of my
idea stand up. Wind combs through them
as if pushing curtains back, and I see
various trees and a sly mountain.

The mountain is what I don't know.
It stands over me, ominous sometimes
in its silent snow, has a trail for goats
to wander up, a ragged trail full of
potholes, and a cool, dancing river.

The river runs right through what I
don't know, invites me in for a dip.
One toe, another, and a shiver goes
up my back. What I don't know is
getting deep now, and by nightfall I
might be afraid. But still I walk in,

knowing I'll never see the full
view in this waking world.

Ah, but the water, the buoyancy
when I stop resisting the flow.
The river in what I don't know
holds me up, prepares me
for the complicated climb.

R. Suzanne Zeitman

Rising to Adjust

From childhood on I felt both a desire and an inner directive to write but was too unaccepting of myself to fathom how to start. Although several experiences in my life passed beyond the boundaries of what I view as normal or safe, only the death of my daughter was an event powerful enough to split time into *before* and *after*, where *after* has no limits on pain or unfairness.

My style of grieving has been bitter, sarcastic, and also complicated by feeling guilty, not for time spent studying or working away from my daughter, but for not enjoying her as much as I could have because I had grown up fearing motherhood as a threat to fulfillment. I have done most of my crying in dreams—dreams that often ended with the thought *I can't stand it*, sometimes followed by *There must be something I can do—that I can control—to make it better*. The only answer I remember getting is

Write.

Somehow I began. I learned to force myself to make awful drafts while waiting for inspiration. It always helps to put your feelings down and a little farther away on paper, but writing helps me mostly, I think, because there is justice in doing what you are supposed to do.

Bareback Riding

I never forgot the sensation of riding bareback, the rhythm of horse and rider moving together. As a child that kind of balance seemed easy and natural. But at this age I have to consider my mischievous old horse and his occasional habit of going up and down rather than forward. Adults tend to calculate the number of days off it takes to heal. They know what can happen and that it happens to them. Yet even the sight of horses can sometimes trick me into thinking the world is a wonderful place.

I remember one night, in particular, when this tricky feeling became so intense it spread out from me into the aisle between the stalls, which was already crowded with horses and riders tacking up. It must have had something to do with the classical music still playing on the radio since, for once, the adults had kept the kids from changing the station. The horses were expert at making known their likes and dislikes, but had yet to indicate any musical tastes, leaving us free to argue about what kind of music they liked best. And though I secretly feared that my horse preferred more popular fare, I couldn't help but respond to the current blend of symphony and emotion with an even greater sense of well-being. Just as music and feeling together seemed to peak and fill the remaining space, I had the bizarre notion that we humans were oblivious and insignificant beasts, while the horses were exalted beings who knew and understood the course of the universe. At the instant this peculiar insight became a conscious thought, my horse turned his head around and nuzzled me.

So I wasn't entirely surprised by the look of acknowledgment I saw in his eye when I finally did ride him bareback and bent his neck slightly to ask him to canter. After the first few strides, I noted gratefully how careful he was to move smoothly. Then it was back again, the rocking and oneness, that childhood combination of riding a roller coaster and loving your pet. Somehow the experience of it forced me to admit I was still foolish enough to keep pricking up my ears and arching my neck in anticipation of a treat, even when I hadn't had one for a while.

Puppet Show

Think of a brown plastic horse.
He Walks! He Eats!
it says on the box
in both English and German.
Push on his back, and his neck
stretches true to life for grazing.
Look how his head
extends naturally when he is led.
Friction alone makes his legs move,
and gears inside do the work.
Life can be this simple.

Then think of a man
who is jealous of puppets,
and me being melted and molded already.
Watch how I follow, and glide
right over the rub of conviction.
He wants to make sure there was no life before him,
so he puts my mechanical horse on a trash heap.

Now I ask in the toy stores of
New York and Munich.
Es läuft! Es frisst! I explain.
And the answer I'm given
is always the same one—
that nothing so wonderful
can ever be found again.

Absolute Proof

Angels emerge
in a tabloid account
of reports only recently
leaked to the West
in which cosmonauts witness
a brilliant orange cloud
that fades to reveal
giant humanlike figures
whose glimmering smiles
boast a glorious secret.

In Atlanta a man
of unbearable sadness
hits his son and his daughter
on their heads with a hammer,
then puts them face down
in the bathtub to die.
A note says he's saved them
the grief of a lifetime
by giving them less than
five minutes of pain.
He's certain that God
will take care of his children.

Sometimes an event
so unusual happens
even tight-lipped astronomers
admit they are nervous.
NASA charts seven angels
as they fly in formation.
Computer-enhanced pictures
are sent to the Vatican,
where according to sources
the sightings resemble
angels of light
as referred to by Paul.

Expert on occult
claims that Satan manifests
in lightning displays
over midwestern cities.
Holocaust deniers
perform home experiments
with rabbits and exhaust fumes,
intended to show that
such gases could not
have been used to kill Jews.

Beings of light surround
bodies of two murdered children.
A star doubles in brightness.
Massive solar eruptions
may be responsible,
but angels are as likely
as any other explanation.

To the Angels of the Supermarket

Blessed are the brain-damaged
who can still find a job
retrieving shopping carts.
This may be true, but
as a student of oafish walks
and simple smiles, I know that
injury is difficult to measure.
Even now I can see the meter
recording your intracranial pressure,
and hear the nurse answer questions
with *These kids do well.*

Thinking you might never have
healed enough to feed yourself
was comfort at the funeral.
But today you appear
by bright boxes of Kid Cuisine
to remind me how you loved
the circulars describing weekly specials,
and how well you could read them at four.
Standing next to bags of cheddar Goldfish,
I remember the card that said
God needed a little angel.

So many empty carts are left
unattended in the parking lot.
I watch the dragging leg
of a gangly young woman
who stops everyone to tell them
tomorrow is her day off.
The uncensored joy on her face
could be taken as a sign
that she is doing well.
Bless her, and bless all of us
who still wonder what that means.

Random Thoughts

Whenever I get on a plane it crashes.
I see the smiles of the stewardesses
and know they don't have the visions,
don't see them every time like I do.

Just like when I'm alone at home,
even snug in bed with a book
and wiggling my toes under soft flannel sheets,
I'm aware of the figures outside.
I know that they're watching
with insular eyes set in cherubic faces
and flexing long fingers that would
smash your head with a club
easier than you could swat a fly.

They don't care how smart you are
or how many degrees you have
or what kind of a contribution
you might make to society.

They don't care if terrible things
have happened to you already
and any human judge would give you a break.
Once you've seen them they stay there,
lurking at the window,
ready to shoot and kill without aiming.

Rising to Adjust

The cat no longer bathes,
and though in her youth
she amused us with play,
at twenty she entertains
with survival
and a curious ability
to maintain integrity
under matted fur.

The aged horse seems healthy,
but like everything I love,
threatens to die at any moment.
Our parents are dead
or talk of dying.
Our child was killed
almost ten years ago.

My mother still laughs
at the description of my family
I wrote in first grade.
I have a dog.
I have a mother.
I have a father.
How innocent that registry
of eventual extinction
seemed at the time.

We dine with friends
while a fish
in the tank by the table
wriggles violently, head at the top,
as though trying to escape.
The host interrupts
our convivial banter
by rising to adjust

the chemistry of the water,
which he admits had at one time
been much too acidic.
This divine intervention
only shocks the fish
into a spurt
of normal swimming,
and soon he returns
to his frantic activity.
Clearly damaged, remarks the hostess.

The next morning we have pancakes
and read of mothers who kill babies
and children who kill each other.
My husband clears the dishes,
then carefully removes the label
from the empty bottle of maple syrup
before placing it in the recycling bin.

At the grocery store
the only available cart
has a specially attached
seat for a baby.
For bereaved parents, I joke.
Everyone's saying, look at them,
such a long time and they're still nuts—
shopping with an empty child carrier.

We stop at a fruit and vegetable stand,
where I recall the surprise
of my first taste of fresh tomatoes,
grown in my great-grandmother's garden.
At home, we eat tomato and cucumber
salad, sitting on the patio,
while the cat at our feet
basks in the unyielding sun.

Advice in Plain English

It began with a book
on cat care and behavior
that said blinking
is a feline expression of love,
then hours of concentration
nose to nose with my cat,
slowly closing my eyes
and waiting for an answer.

Later, when the robin
I tried to save died,
I should have realized
it wasn't that simple.
Was I wrong
to keep a sick bird in a shoe box
without being sure what to feed it?
And the day in high school

when my English teacher, Miss Carey,
had a breakdown
and described to the class
her affair with a mechanic,
what lesson was she trying to give?

Now I view cats
as solitary creatures,
and find inspiring accounts—
like the story of a cat
bravely dragging her kittens
from a burning garage—
unnerving, like the volume of letters
from Sylvia Plath to her mother,
that puzzling testimony
to the bonds of singed fur
published after Plath's suicide.

Now I sympathize
with tales of failed romances,
even tonight, as our guest,
my husband's young student,
shares the details of her love life
with engaging sincerity
enhanced by perky breasts
and a self-absorption
excusable in kittens.

I remember what it's like
to be drinking Jack Daniel's
one night by the river
and hear how beautiful my breasts are.
I remember what it's like when it's over
to hear *Don't be like that. Don't cry.*
But whose fault is it?
Plath was sick before
she married Ted Hughes,
before the jealousy and burned letters,
before the rage and separation.

When a woman is seductive,
my father warned,
a man can't help himself.
A tail held to one side
is a sexual invitation.
And while my husband sees
his student's disclosures
as a gesture of friendship,
I've seen a cat play with food.

Yet Miss Carey was wrong
to look directly at me
as she ended her monologue

by saying *You must understand*,
since even now I can't reply
to the torment in her eyes,
I can't explain
why a cat
who never goes out in the road
suddenly runs right in front of a car,
or why a woman
sticks her head in an oven and dies
while her children are safe
in their bedroom upstairs.

And when the student turns to me
for a token response,
though I've been in her place
enough to know why to fear her,
though I've found—and written—
letters from the other woman,
I remain without an answer
for either of us.

Temporary Tales

A soporific dread builds
as I walk down the grocery aisles.
The cats need special food.
The pain medication doesn't work.
She uses fabric softener and I don't.
Her bottom is sore from the wheelchair.
But this time she'll get better.

It's only temporary after all.
Long ago we took trips to the park
so I could pretend to be Snow White and
flee through the woods from the huntsman
till collapsing in exhaustion and despair.
But now I keep safe from my mother
just by hypnotizing whatever in me
she finds threatening.

It's the deep sleep I hate most.
Sometimes, in my dreams, she is dying.
Don't worry, I plead,
I'll remember how beautiful you were.
I dream of how she said
I wasn't pretty, and all I tell her is
It's all right, we'll change places.

Is anybody who they were before anyway?
In the first version of Snow White,
it was her real mother, you know.
Driving away from the store,
I see an old woman out walking.
Her steps are measured and powerless.
I open the door and there is my mother,
trapped in her wheelchair and so glad to see me.
Wake up! Wake up! I tell myself,
and kiss her before the ending.

Hymn to Hysteria

Once there was a curse
from woman to woman.
We lay in grey chambers
obscured by sick shadows
when the chorus announced
the birth of our daughters.

We took care of our dolls,
fed them taproots and Tampax,
dressed them in outfits
smelling of powder and sex,
waited for soft real mouths to
emerge from their hard rubber faces.

Sunrise was for scavenging,
midday for masquerades,
and late-night for lullabies
from the shocking side of mother.
Our striped legs protruded from
under houses that crushed us.

Disciples and dilettantes,
we thrashed out a passage
to where we hated to travel,
just to slink back at last
to our cradles and the crooning
that soothed us and made us sing along.

       Give us a charm with the secret of healing
       contagion from those we are born to caress.
       Give us three teats and a spot without feeling.
       Intensity serves as a kind of success.

The Ugly Sister

I am the sister that you don't remember,
although I have been your protector and match.
With our limbs interlaced in the darkness of bedtime,

I was the one who gave out the warning
never to put your foot over the edge.

I am the sister you've never forgotten,
the one that you fear may show up in dark mirrors.
I am the sister who knows a good story

of what can be found when you turn over beauty.
Hear me reveal how we came by our looks.

I had no choice but to go along with you,
flapping our arms and pretending to fly,
jumping from chairs in a superman outfit.

I had no choice but to trip and fall with you.
I am the sister that you never had.

But on the hard floor, as we waited for rescue,
you studied the red sight of blood from our forehead,
while I heard the screams that failed to come closer.
And on the cold table, as stitches were made,
you examined the paper that shielded our eyes,
while I heard the sobs about scarring for life.

By the time we were ten, your scar was invisible,
but mine had expanded till my eyes were uneven
and my face was a portrait of all we find hideous.
You've seen me in dreams, as the maimed try to touch you,
longing to make you as loathsome as they are.
I am their captain, who just craves your attention.

Moment

I suppose it's lonely beauty
that makes time stand still.
The view is shimmering snow
framed between the reddish
brown ears of my horse.
To me at thirteen,
such quiet is striking.

Each breath makes me conscious
of the crispness of living.
The warm walking beneath me
performs the usual magic of animals,
convincing me that the universe
is proceeding as it should

although, in truth, much is wrong.
The owner of the stable fondles
young girls, and the groom with a
pimply-faced wife and six children
will soon try to hang himself.
The life I think I have
will start to crumble.

But now the sky is so steely blue
it seems solid as I ride
past the white fence and bare trees
out onto the undisturbed trails.

Early Tragedy

According to Aristotle,
there is a beginning,
middle and end, a dose
of recognition, a hero
of sufficient stature
with a flaw (if that really is
the proper translation).
While others find escape
in looking back at the beginning,
my memories of young life
are film clips made, amazingly,
before the person playing me arrives,
full of action, nonetheless,
in which my shape keeps changing
as it struggles for applause.

There were, of course,
sparks of awareness, when
common words flashed in my mind
as though I'd never heard them,
or when pain alone was able
to flesh out my skeleton identity.
So I can relive the terror
of waiting for a boyfriend
with a Librium in my hand
to tone down the agony
if he doesn't show up.
So I can recall the chatter
from the TV in my room,
which was on all the time
to drown out the worry
that I'd done something wrong.

And in the hours of stillness
and prophecy, when the pattern
of life was the late-night movie,

it was the ill-starred women
with whom I identified,
for I'd come to fear the ordinary,
without knowing the consequences
or the fact that only sorrow
is fundamental enough
to be felt before it happens.
So I trembled at the story
of an old woman waking
from a forty-year coma.
So I cried at the scene
of a crazy woman rocking
a doll in place of her lost child.

And the heroes I remember
were animals, like the mistreated horse
I loved but couldn't rescue,
trotting with proud and starving beauty,
or kittens I saw at a pet shop,
whose future years of purring and energy
were on sale for ten dollars,
so much good life for so little.
The best—if not the proper—
translation of *hamartia*
came from a shrink
who defined it as my inability
to say how I wanted my coffee
or to partake of the warm-hearted
permission we need for existence.

And now that *self* is a word
with a meaning I can feel
and I'm ready for roles

of youth and seduction,
I find in the mirror
an aging woman still haunted,
not by greatness falling,
but by the misery of a child
who is loved yet not enjoyed,
not by a complex plot,
but by the missed chance,
the wistful hope
that comes in soft moments
for what I know
to be irretrievably lost.

To Live For

I'm as young as I remember
and shrieking in terror
the first time my parents
go somewhere without me.
But the world doesn't end
when the door shuts behind them.
Instead, I turn to my grandmother
and ask for a story.

A girl once married a gentleman
who gambled away everything
except the baby and wedding dress.
Father came to the rescue,
saving her and the baby,
but made her leave the dress behind.
    There's something to be said
    for having a meal on the table.

A husband dined in his undershirt
while his wife stood and watched.
Then at night, while he slept,
she sneaked downstairs
to snack on tomato sandwiches
and read novels on the couch.
    Find what it is that you're
    not afraid to die doing.

I'm as old as my grandmother
and heir to her passion
for tomato sandwiches.
Everything frightens me—
though I feel brave on a horse,
having made a deal long ago.
I'll buy a young and wild one—
as soon as I'm too tired for stories.

Tamara Graham

Burying the Dogwood

I was dreaming again, driving alone in a fast red sports car late at night, racing to get back home before something unspeakable happened.

I was breathing too much and too fast, and not getting enough air, as the realization hit me that I was about to die. Not on some eventual distant day in my future, but soon, suddenly. With the foreknowledge that only the dreamer can have, I saw the party I'd just left and the cyanide pill dropped into my drink by some unknown predator. I didn't know why or when; I was only certain that when the plastic coating of the capsule containing the poison was eroded by my stomach acid, I was as good as dead.

So instead of stopping the car, I began to pray. I think when push comes to shove, it was to the Methodist god I prayed—at least that's the image I hold in my mind. But regardless of who I prayed to, it came from the depths of my soul. I still remember the stink of fear in the car and my frantic desperation. The most amazing part was that I was convinced someone was actually listening.

I told the Methodist god that if he let me live, I would promise to stay. Stay in my marriage, that is. I would stay in this relationship, even if it killed me, if only he would let me live.

And so, in the magical way of dreams, the cyanide pill popped up into my mouth, as if by hydraulic pressure, ready for inspection. As I pulled the capsule from my lips, I knew the condition of the plastic coating would tell the story. If the coating was clean and unspoiled, I'd live. If it was damaged by stomach acid, I was destined to be under a marker in some southern Methodist cemetery.

The capsule was half eaten away.

My first thought as I stared at the bedroom ceiling was, "Oh, shit, I'm dead," which was quickly followed by, "Oh, shit, I'm alive." I thought I'd just made a promise I would live to regret. Fortunately, I didn't honor it.

But I did carry the guilt around until I picked up my pen and began to write. I thought for years that I'd broken a pledge, when instead the dream had been a message, a blessing even, to leave.

I kept a dream journal for a while after that. Of all my initial forays into writing, dream writing was by far the most interesting. It wasn't written for anyone's eyes but my own—fragmented thoughts, images, snatches of visions—it sometimes didn't make sense. But what fun it was to see the images and stories and problems I would try to solve at night. I've since learned to pay attention to these nocturnal wanderings.

That led to keeping a journal for two years, just like when I was eleven and writing my secrets into a cheap green vinyl diary. The adult version turned out to be mostly whining, which is not to say it was a bad thing. At least my family and friends didn't have to listen day after day, although they couldn't escape from me entirely. In fact, now that I think about it, it was a family member who suggested journaling as an alternative to boring my friends to death. Since I still have a few friends left, it must have worked.

So now I grab a moment between planes, or at Burger King, or after my son is asleep, and I write. Sometimes it's worthy of editing, most times it's not. Sometimes it's just stream of consciousness, and on some rare occasions, it's actually profound.

But mostly, it's just fun. I haven't dreamed of cyanide pills in a very long time, although I occasionally still have visions of fast red sports cars. But in the latest installment, I'm driving on the beach in a convertible with the top down, and the sun is shining on my face.

Grandmama

I dreamed I gave birth to an owl last night. I called out to Grandmama once, that I knew it was a girl, and then she appeared, effortlessly sliding into the world on her powerful wings. I asked Grandmama if this meant that I had finally achieved wisdom, and she said, "No, girl, you can't claim that until you've truly lived."

Once, when she was four, living on that Polk County dirt farm long since gone to seed, her brother Burch convinced her that if she would climb the sty and grab a pig, something wonderful would happen.

"Essie, you grab Beulah tight around the front legs," Burch said. "Oma and I will hold her down for you and then, if you suck hard on her teat, I promise you, you'll see the wind blow." Her sister said, "Essie, you'll truly see the wind blow, but you have to suck really hard." Grandmama tied her long dress up around her waist, climbed the sty, rolled in the mud once or twice, and grabbed Beulah. I never heard her tell exactly what it felt like, but I've always remembered her description of the wind. Of course, so have Burch and Oma, since she convinced them to jump in the mud with her and try it out for themselves.

When Granddaddy died, she was forty-nine and Mama was twenty-two. While Mama fell quietly apart, Grandmama loudly made plans. Before long, she'd taken in a boarder, opened a grocery store, closed a grocery store, opened a carpet store, closed a carpet store, and sold chenille bedspreads by the side of the road on the way to Dalton. "What do you mean, you don't need a new bedspread, of course you need a new bedspread, think of your husband, children, neighbors, dog." There are families all over north Georgia and east Tennessee with a Beckler bedspread or carpet, thanks to Grandmama's muleheadedness.

When she got bored, which was often, she'd do just about anything to stir things up. As I was trying on the last of many wedding dresses for the marriage that was best remembered for the reception, she decided she'd had enough. "Excuse me, I'm having a heart attack," she said to the saleslady, and lay down on the floor in the middle of the bridal salon at the downtown Richs. As Mama and

I stepped over her, the saleslady peered at her oddly, and then cautiously took an awkward step over her, too. I chose my first wedding dress over the prone body of a seventy-seven-year-old woman. It was the most beautiful thing about that wedding.

When I divorced, she was angry. First at me, because "Tammy, darling, you've always got your nose in a damn book. Pay more attention to your man and everything will come out alright." But when it was clear that, books aside, this marriage was doomed, she accepted it, decided it was his fault, and moved on. When I decided, as all recently divorced women do, never to marry again, I cried in her arms about being childless. "So what's the big deal, Tammy? You go to the clinic, you pick out a good match and get yourself artificially inseminated. Marriage is overrated, anyhow. I've loved being single; I can fart when I feel like it, and leave the bathroom door open anytime I want."

She wasn't there for me to step over when I picked out my second wedding dress, and she's never seen the baby I had in the traditional way. But sometimes, when I'm alone, I leave the bathroom door open and think of her. I think of wings, and power, and beauty and strength. I hope I dream of owls again tonight. Maybe Grandmama will tell me what it means.

Bacon as Love

It's possible that my family is fixated on pigs. Certainly, my mother went through a phase of pigmania, collecting pigs of every variety: ceramic pigs, outdoor garden pigs, teapot pigs, refrigerator magnet pigs, doorstopper pigs, even toilet-roll holder pigs. And of course, Grandmama had experienced an intimate relationship with pigs at an early age.

However, long before Mama began collecting pigs, they were an essential part of our morning routine. Every morning of my childhood, she rose early and cooked a full breakfast for my father and me. I would lie in bed and the smell of frying bacon would drift slowly upstairs, searching for my nose buried deep in the white cotton sheets. We never needed an alarm clock in those days. Mama's breakfast bacon was very reliable.

I would come padding down the stairs, and Mama would have everything on the table: the juice, the one piece of Roman Meal buttered toast, the scrambled egg—and the bacon. Sometimes, for variety, she would add half a grapefruit or a dollop of buttered grits, but the bacon never varied. She always set the table backwards—the fork on the right, and the knife and spoon on the left. This made sense to me, as the majority of the world is right-handed, until I married. We argued relentlessly over this point, until I reluctantly consulted *The Joy of Cooking*. I submit that proper etiquette may require a fork positioned on the left, but reasonable and efficient diners place them on the right. I'm sure Mama would agree.

There were unspoken rites of passage in this breakfast ritual. Scrambled eggs were always part of the routine, until one morning when I was in the eighth grade. I descended the stairs to spy a round, wrinkled thing on my plate. It looked out of place at my usual chair; perhaps Daddy hadn't left for work, and this was his breakfast plate. It couldn't possibly be mine. When Mama calmly said good morning over her cup of coffee, I knew something had changed when I wasn't looking.

Obviously, sometime during the night, I had passed a threshold of sorts. The fried egg had traditionally been reserved for the adults in the family, but I had now reached the age of reason. Jewish girls have the Bat Mitzvah; girls in my family have the fried egg.

Bacon was part of my life from infancy until I left home for college. Sure, there were a few rebellious mornings. "No, Mom, I don't have time for this fattening breakfast," or when I really wanted to hurt her, "Mom, we aren't farmers anymore." Fortunately, she never listened to me, and by and large, most mornings began with this rich, salty, enveloping aroma.

Bacon got a bad reputation in the 80's, high in fat, nitrates, cholesterol and the like. I began to eat bagels and drink black coffee in the morning, in an attempt to gain cosmopolitan sophistication. It didn't work, although there is something to be said for consistency. I know Mama would agree.

I've since married a man who doesn't eat breakfast, and most mornings are too rushed to cook bacon anyway. But the smell of those thin, frying slices of pork automatically takes me back to times of safety and comfort—lazy mornings with people who love me unconditionally. I sure do miss those days. I haven't smelled anything even remotely close to bacon in a long, long time.

Mama Said

You see more people in the grocery
than you do at the movies,
so never wear plastic hair rollers
in public.

Present your best face when you open the door.
You don't know who's on the other side, she said.
So never open the door
in a flowered house coat.

And she wore orange chiffon sometimes,
which looked wonderful,
even though *Color Me Beautiful*
said it was not her season.

Only reds and blacks and vibrant colors
for a winter personality, the book said,
but the author didn't know Mama.

Sometimes she just let the doorbell ring and ring.

Effie Lee

Aunt Effie Lee died last Thursday. It wasn't unexpected, as she was nearly eighty-nine years old, sick and almost bent double with a bad case of osteoporosis. She'd been in an old folks home up by the Nottely River for the last eight years, and it wasn't a bad place as such places go. They took good care of her, but her mind was going by the time she got there, and by the time I finally got around to visiting, it was completely gone.

During that one uncomfortable visit, she peered up at me from her hospital bed, roughly camouflaged with white chintz pillows and a flowered spread, and I thought I saw a glimmer of recognition in her eyes. But it was false hope; she was only curious about who had entered her room, and she quickly fell back into her own private reverie, where mountain deer cavorted around her bedside and her long dead husband asked her to dance a slow waltz.

○ ○ ○

One hot Sunday afternoon in late July, Effie Lee and Grandmama decided to go berry picking on Samuel Riser's farm. Samuel had rented two of his farmhouses to them, and he lived down the road about a half-mile. Samuel had never married; he lived with his mother until she died, and then he took over the farm. He was not an unpleasant man, but he looked a little disheveled, and his hair was always in need of a trim. Every day for fifteen years, he could be seen dragging rocks in a rusty wheelbarrow, adding to the stone memorial he was building for his mother. No one was exactly sure what the memorial was supposed to be, although it resembled the Great Wall of China. But the building of it gave him purpose, and he wasn't dangerous, so everyone complimented his work to his face, and then quietly laughed, not unkindly, when he wasn't around.

He gave the two women permission to pick blackberries that day, but neglected to mention that there were swampy pits just beyond the lines of his property. They had picked enough berries for a pie or two, when Effie Lee suddenly let go with a high-pitched scream that frightened the crows out of the trees. Grandmama looked behind her just in time to see Effie Lee slide down into the ground. As she kept sliding and screaming, Grandmama finally realized that Effie Lee was caught in the quicksand. She turned around to run. "Effie Lee, stay there," she yelled over her shoulder, as if Effie Lee were going anywhere. "I'll get help."

At that, Effie Lee's voice, usually so cultured and refined, boomed loud enough to be heard across two counties. "Essie Nevada, you get your butt back here this minute and pull me out of this mess, or I'll never speak to you again, so help me God!" Fortunately for Effie Lee, Grandmama broke with tradition and did as she was told.

Effie Lee lived close to Grandmama most of her life. When Grandmama's people came down the mountain from Polk County, they settled near Effie Lee in Eton's red clay valley. Grandmama was already twenty-one, considered an old maid by some, and a little wild by mountain standards. Before Effie Lee's brother had a chance to understand what was happening, he was married to Grandmama and living in a white clapboard house next to his mama and daddy and Effie Lee on the Chatsworth Road.

The two sisters-in-law couldn't have been more different. Effie Lee was considered well-read and refined. Grandmama had no use for books or formal education of any kind. Grandmama could sell ice to the Eskimos, and Effie Lee could hardly bear to deal with tradespeople at all. Grandmama was a bull in a china shop; Effie Lee was a porcelain doll.

But somehow, they became friends. When Grandmama discovered she was pregnant, the first person she told was Effie Lee.

"I'll make you a deal," she said, as they sipped coffee at Grandmama's scarred oak kitchen table. "If you come look after me and the baby when it's born, I promise to do the same for you when your first baby comes."

Effie Lee agreed, and when the baby was born, she cooked her new husband a few dinners to tide him over, and moved in to help out for a time. Grandmama was useless; she had no idea of what to do with a baby, and she was nervous and ill-tempered. Effie Lee took charge in her efficient way; she cooked meals, washed clothes, changed diapers, cleaned the kitchen, and rocked the baby to sleep most nights.

Of course, when Effie Lee's first baby came, Grandmama was nowhere to be found. She was likely to have made some excuse about the family back in Tennessee needing her, but Effie Lee had to fend for herself. It wouldn't be the last time such a thing happened.

When Eton started feeling the pinch of the Great Depression, it was Effie Lee who led the family out of the mountains. Many of them were intimidated by the big city, but Effie Lee packed her husband a suitcase and sent Lloyd off to find work in the factories of Detroit. Granddaddy stayed behind because he had a small income as the Eton chief of police. Since the town was too strapped for cash to provide him with a gun or a car, the successful criminals in Eton were those who could outrun my granddaddy.

Lloyd stayed in Detroit only long enough to work his way back home. After he returned, Granddaddy resigned his position and they all moved to Cedar Grove, near Samuel Riser's farm. They lived off the land for a while, and the two families shared a cow named Mabel, a pig named Beulah (in honor of Grandmama), a few chickens and a summer garden. And ate the occasional berry pie.

Effie Lee and Grandmama raised children together, celebrated every Christmas Eve together their entire lives, buried their husbands together. They had an argument every once in awhile, even went one whole year without speaking. I don't remember the reason—something about a family quilt or scrapbook. But they always made up and vowed to be friends forever.

When Grandmama came down with what turned out to be her final illness, it was Effie Lee who sat by her bedside, and read Bible stories to her late into the night. Grandmama was not an easy patient; but Effie Lee cooked special meals for her, brought glasses of water, wiped her brow, prayed with her, cried for her. When Grandmama went kicking and screaming into the hereafter, it was Effie Lee who held her hand.

Last Wednesday night, I stopped by the nursing home for a few minutes, knowing it was likely to be my last visit.

She seemed to be asleep as I sat down in the blue vinyl chair closest to the bed. After a while, listening to the rhythmic sounds of her labored breathing, I found myself drifting off. Suddenly, I snapped awake to see Effie Lee sitting upright and clear-eyed in her bed. She turned her head toward the window and said loudly, "Essie Nevada, you get your butt over here and get me out of this mess right now!" and then she began to laugh, a great belly laugh that came right up from her old, arthritic toes.

That was the last time I saw her. The viewing was held this week back home in Eton, underneath the stuffed grizzly bear at JD's funeral parlor. It seemed a perfectly fitting farewell. As strange as JD's collection of stuffed boar, piranha and knives seemed to the younger members of the family, they've never lived in Eton. After all, JD knows his business better than anyone else. For forty years, he's met the taxidermy needs, as well as handled the funerals of most everyone in town.

We buried her two rows over from Grandmama. They're not too far from the old home place on the Chatsworth Road. And the Eton Primitive Baptist Church still honors the tradition of dinner on the grounds every so often. They would like that. Maybe I'll drive up and have fried chicken and potato salad and a piece of berry pie with them some Sunday afternoon.

Preserved

He asked me one day,
as we were walking along the northern shoreline,
What are wild berries, Mama?
and I thought it such an odd question.

In halting words, I explained
the growth patterns of old forest
and the differences between
black and red and blue and raspberries,

and the variety of fruits
in different geological regions
of North America
that foster berry growth.

He looked at me in confusion and
then laughed with the certainty of youth.
He said, *No, Mama, you're wrong.*
That's not what wild berries are.

Wild berries tickle,
and they dance when you're not looking.
They tell bad jokes
and sing silly songs.

I laughed out loud,
They throw things
where they're not supposed to,
and they trip each other on the way

to important meetings.
They spin and roll
and chase each other
in the woods late at night.

Wild berries
should take Ritalin
but they don't
because then they would be tame.

Running toward the surf
with wild and tangled hair,
he shouted back over his shoulder,
And who wants to grow up to be jam, anyway?

Under Pressure

All the people at work
are off and running,
except for me.

And when the Chairman arrives,
I am in bed.
I look over at the bed
next to mine
and there is the guy
who was fired last week.

He has no excuse.
Mine?
It's been a rough couple of days.

I. Packing for Vancouver

My anxieties are well traveled, you see. They've been to the beach, the Appalachian mountains, Chicago, San Francisco, and now British Columbia. They're not as well traveled as I am—there once was a time when I traveled alone, but lately they seem to be the first thing I pack. Even before the black suitcase and maroon garment bag are hauled out of the closet, they're all lined up, clamoring to be taken along.

Yesterday I flew over two thousand miles—squeezed in between an undersized man with an oversized laptop and an elderly woman who talked nonstop for five hours about how enzyme therapy had changed her life—just to get to the top of this mountain. I can't remember now why it was so important, and I wonder why I find myself surprised that I'm not alone.

I have a fear—not a big one, mind you, just a nagging doubt—that someday my anxiety will grow so huge that someone in my family will say, "Okay, that's it, off to Milledgeville you go." As everyone in south Georgia knows, Milledgeville is the euphemism for, and the location of, the famous mental institution.

I've always felt sorry for anyone who really was from Milledgeville—there's a huge difference between being *from* Milledgeville and being *in* Milledgeville, but even so, having the town as your home base is always slightly suspect. Like Cindy Frazier, my college roommate. I think it's likely her protruding eyes and edgy nervousness stemmed from an overactive thyroid, but she had the misfortune to be from Milledgeville, and so her fate was sealed. She dropped out after the first semester, ostensibly overwhelmed by the workload, but in reality, wounded by the titters and whispers she couldn't help but hear behind her back.

So here I am, driving up a Canadian mountain far from Milledgeville, Georgia, winding past Horseshoe Bay and Fuzzy Creek, listening to hits from the 60's and 70's. The radio announcer suddenly informs me that one out of five British Columbians will suffer from some form of mental illness in his or her lifetime. I've met only six people so far: the customs official at the airport, the cabbie, the hotel clerk, and three clearly unstable people on Water Street. Based on the one out of five rule, I'm entitled to meet nine mentally sturdy people today. I wonder if they'll find me.

II. Tripping

This morning, eating a bacon, egg and cheese biscuit at the McDonald's in the Vancouver subway, I glance up at the sound of heavy, plodding feet. A young man has bypassed a handful of embarrassed diners to make a beeline for my table. He has a most beautiful face, bright blue eyes burning with either innocence or fever. I realize that he's just a boy.

"You know, they don't like it when I tip the garbage cans," he says firmly. The other diners begin sneaking looks at us, as he hops first on one foot, then the other. I can't tear my eyes from his burning face.

"I don't understand it, the food is just as good in the can as it is at your table, but they get so mad." His voice rises slightly at the ends of his sentences.

I feel something give in my chest as I notice how dirty he is. He has on a baseball cap advertising some unknown sports franchise. The grime on the brim is thick, and his jeans are a sour greenish color, encrusted with dirt and what looks like mold. But his face is so pure and so beyond my reach that I can only think of how his mother must cry at night for him.

"I do okay, you know, but sometimes I get so hungry." Again, that lilt at the end of his sentence. I keep forgetting I'm in Canada, and it sounds like he's pleading with me.

I reach into my purse and pull out five dollars. "Please, go get yourself something to eat," I say quickly. His bright blue eyes burn hotter for a moment, and he looks directly at me for the first time. "You gotta stop worrying," he says with conviction. "Nobody can ever really hurt you."

Then his eyes cloud over once again. "Mum," he says haltingly, then shakes his head. "No, no, Aunt Eleanor." He stops again. "I'll tell Mum what you did for me," he says as he wanders off. I watch him as he finds a spot in line, talking to himself. I watch him as the others in line slowly edge away from him to avoid contamination. It's that one out of five rule, you see—the twenty percent might infect the rest. I wonder if Aunt Eleanor cries at night for him, too.

When I look up after taking a bite of greasy egg biscuit, he's disappeared. I'm surprised that he's able to move so fast after getting his food, and I actually stand up to get a view of the subway entrance, but he's gone. Completely vanished back into the labyrinth.

The man at the next table speaks frantically into his cell phone, and the woman across from me speed-types on her laptop. I throw my half-eaten breakfast into the trash bin and walk slowly past the already harried commuters jogging to their offices. And later in the morning, I drive slowly and calmly up into the mountains, weaving my way between cars engaged in the mad competitive race to beat the next traffic light.

Backstroke in Campbell's Soup

It's cream of mushroom
with black bits floating just below the surface,
sticking to my eyelashes
and nostrils,
as I methodically
swim back and back and back and
I'm losing count of the strokes,
I can't breathe anymore,
my eyes and ears and nose,
every opening that had feeling
is closed now,
covered with Campbell's clots of curdled cream
and I'm sinking to the bottom,
but oh, so slowly.

I can't recall how I got to this place,
but it was probably my own fault,
allowing myself to be convinced
that the label on the can made me safe.

And it would help so much
if someone would just add water and stir
or even turn the heat up.
Perhaps I would jump out like a scalded frog
or maybe, unknowing, boil to death.

If I could only climb out of this viscous sludge,
I would go back to gazpacho and vichyssoise again,
often eaten alone and
best served cold.

Crossings

I tell that old woman
with the canyons in her face
to teach me how to drive the car,
not how to build it.

And Mama says,
you can take a hot air balloon
all the way from New York to Florida now.
It goes faster and faster
the further south you get.

But I choose to drive over the mountain,
flying over potholes and racing
over icy roads, near misses, and close quarters
to the town I've seen in my dreams,
the town with Christmas wreaths
and tiny lights in all the windows.
But the restaurant's closed and all my friends are gone.

Somewhere, somebody says,
Pick up those abandoned toys
left in the parking lot for the children.
Don't leave them out.

I drive by once, slowly,
cautiously weighing the options,
yet leaving the rocking horse,
the doll babies and the fairy tales
further and further behind.

I have to go back,
do it all over again in reverse,
watching images on my windshield
in scratchy slow motion,
babies reentering the womb,
lovers walking backwards through door after door,
wives taking rings off their fingers
and cars driving backwards
across the mountain towards home.

Dogwoods

The dogwood tree in my front yard is weak and spindly looking. It may have something to do with being planted in Yankee soil or maybe all northern dogwoods look like mine. It stands by the front walk, wedged between the cement and the brick walls of the house, slightly leaning into the second story window. I always feel guilty when I walk by, like there's some brand of Southern magic I can perform to make it healthy again.

Grandmama had the finest dogwood tree in north Georgia. It had branches low enough to the ground for a six-year-old to climb on and, in the spring, blossoms and leaves profuse enough to hide in. I loved that tree; my grandfather had planted it long before I was born, and although I never knew him, the tree was a living connection to this quiet man.

I enjoyed the sense of power the tree gave me. I loved to hide among those leaves and watch the neighbors walk by, unaware that they were silently observed. The tree protected me at those times when I was guilty of one thing or another—breaking something, getting sassy at Grandmama's bossiness. Getting sassy was the worst sin imaginable in our family, so I spent quite a few afternoons hiding in that tree.

Once, when I was very small, Grandmama told me the story of how the dogwood tree came to be. About two thousand years ago, around the time that Jesus was preaching his sermons on the mount and changing water into wine, the dogwood was a great, tall, strong tree, similar to a hickory or Southern live oak. When it came time for the crucifixion, the dogwood was chosen to bear the burden of his weight. As he lay dying, the dogwood, in pain at its shameful role in this passion play, shriveled up and became the fragile tree of modest size and twisted limbs that it is today.

But in the spring, at Easter time, it bursts forth with a radiant blossom. As Grandmama told me this story, she took me outside to the tree by the kitchen window. She pulled off a blossom and showed me how, if you view the four petals correctly, a little cross appears in the center with a few bright red drops surrounding it. She said the tree was all about forgiveness. Seems to me it was all about guilt.

I've since planted a dogwood tree at every house I've ever lived in. I bought the first one with the money from my allowance, and Daddy and I planted it together. When I rented my first apartment, I kept dogwood branches in a large ceramic vase on my scarred oak coffee table, and when I married, we planted a dogwood by the back fence of our first house. We planted dogwoods in climates where they were never intended to grow. It became a ritual, even an obsession over the years, at each new place, and they all seemed to thrive as long as I nurtured them.

I didn't have to plant a dogwood tree at the house we live in now; it already came with one. Finding that lonesome, misplaced tree made the decision to move here easier for me. But since the dogwood has begun to die, seems like it might be time to consider moving on again. I'm tired of working so hard to breathe life into something that's going to die anyway. I've used all the nutrients and fertilizers that the nursery can provide; I've talked to the tree, sometimes gently, oftentimes firmly; I even allowed myself to be convinced to hold a Native American birthing ritual in a last ditch effort to save it. But this time, all the nurturing and loving and yearning didn't do any good.

And as for me, well, I don't think I need to plant any more dogwoods. I think it's time to be moving on to a new place, where I can leave off the planting and growing of trees altogether, a place where the dogwoods flourish or die on their own, and Southern magic remains a mystery.

Ann Holdreith

Weightless Birds and Holy Diamonds

Shining

It isn't predictable;
it just happens, like a plum
dropping from a tree.
The heart relaxes,
sheds its chrysalis,
gives up the pretense of safety.
Inner petals slowly open.
Morning light. Pink breathing.
Delicate chambered plum
lets sun touch its skin.
The hard pit in the center yields.
All that remains
is a steady
shining.

Points of Light

I crawl with my belly to the earth,
rain streaked, mud streaked.
I am a naked map
connecting points of light
to point of life
in the lost sky, in the hidden sea,
in the invisible space
beyond the highway's hill,
staircase pointed
to where my eyes have never been.

Morphic fields emit sounds
only peacocks hear.
Octaves beyond keys we touched
and then forgot.
Our black, shiny shoes are sewn
with metal mirrors that ricochet floors,
ricochet walls off ceilings,
ricochet through wide open windows,
through curtains blowing in the hot winds.
Ricochet across points of light,
studded fractals that splinter,
collide and multiply,

keep dancing, keep dancing, keep dancing

connect the dots and make me one.
I am vibrating faster than the sound
only peacocks can hear,

moving, moving, moving
a naked map of the Universe,
a map stretching beyond the Universe,
points of light,
points of light,
point of life.

The New Game

My hormones are out of whack;
I'm doing a big nose-dive.
Get your eyes checked, buddy!
             I scream
when the jerk barges so blatantly,
                right in front of me.
Pull me like silly putty
in a hundred different ways,
              'cause I'll bounce back,
I won't crack,
         sidetrack,
                blow my stack
or even have a heart attack.

O—o—o—o—h—m—m—m, O—o—o—o—h—m—m
Shakti . . . Shiva . . . Holy Mary . . . Jesus . . .

Now, I ain't into blasphemy,
I just need to de-materialize
instantly. Quaker oatmeal,
Lipton soup, chicken pot pies,
grab it off the shelf,
pop it in the wave,
babe, I got you and you got me,
but nobody's got anybody anyhow, so
so stay out of my way,
cause I'M IN A HURRY!

The Industrial Age
has shot its wad,

        information,
        information,
multiplying at the speed of light,
m—m—m—m—m—m—
        m—m—m—
          m—m—m
sex on the web is out of sight.

New Age,
Ice Age,

        poles are tilting,
        ozone's melting,
        earth is raging,
I can't breathe. . . can't breathe. . . can't breathe. . .
and we're all gasping for love—
        all gasping for love—
          gasping for—

love . . .
love . . .
love . . .

Deep in the ethers,
furrowed in the folds of the galaxies,
beyond the outer galaxies—
millions of tiny seed cells,
b—r—e—a—t—h—i—n—g.

Legions of micro-matter wait in the sea,
bathed in the combustive vat of the sea,
brewing, heaving,
bubbling,

b—r—e—a—t—h—i—n—g.

Life explodes in one big bang,
prana ignites inside our spines.
A clear lake shines
in the babe's new eyes,
and we remember
to remember
b—r—e—a—t—h—i—n—g.

Veils of lifetimes fly into the blue.
The buzz in our veins
melts in our minds
and you and me are we
and we are
b—r—e—a—t—h—i—n—g.

Planets converge in an orbit of white.
The sun begins to spin.
All hearts break open
simultaneously,
and we can see everyone
and everything
B—R—E—A—T—H—I—N—G.

Love is who you are, love
is the name of the new game.

Congalese

He's got my drum.
The guy wants to kidnap my drum.
He thinks he can bongo with my congo.
Snatch it in his snare.
Slip it out the back, Jack,
as if I wasn't there.
Beat me to the bar, big Daddy,
your eyes are clouded with mirrors of your own.

I could smell you a mile away,
those eyes that shimmied and bounced
when I came in close to speak your game.
But the game said your heart was big and kind,
your spirit full of passion and fun.
I played fool to myself. I didn't listen . . .
I let you beat my drum!

I ride that drum in a dream;
my legs wrapped around a winged stallion.
We fly through the night into the sun.
We ride in perfect freedom,
the drum beating in my hips and thighs.
I laugh wild into the wind.
I ride with my eyes open wide.

You have my drum, but you do not have me.

I refuse the pitter-patter, the hide and seek,
the in and out, the up and down.
I'm no roller-coaster baby, no yo-yo mamma.
I walk the straight and narrow
that bends and curves to the inner sound . . .
Boom ba ta, boom
It taps out the code I live by,
plants me solid on the ground.

I let that drum go into the night
and see it fly back with wings of its own.
Destroyer angels surround and spin out
all that distorts its sweet sound.
The black boxes of crazy games,
crack inside the spin.

The drum flies straight to its place at my door,
a message beating in its skin.
A new beat
sounds in my heart;
love
is ready to begin.

BOOM - BA - TA - BOOM - BOOM - BOOM

Saints of Another Time

A finger is pointed at the cupboard,
a hand is in the cage.
The pin drops, but no one hears it.

We never saw the pearl inside the glove.
We pretend that everything is fine, our hands
pointing and bound at the same time.

Dance with me in the garden.
Pull me into the quiet of our flesh,
synchronized as we twirl and lift,

saints of another time, perfumed and
anointed with virtue and loss,
our fragments dissolving into the dusk.

You carry only a tablet of white paper.
My hands glide through your hair with
unspoken pearls. The door of the cage

opens. Together, we walk toward the sound
of the ocean, our fingers whispering
prayers that ask to be found.

Wild Perfume

We wince in the mortar of words
deaf on the walls of our tongue
eyelids crust with the soap of tears
moan into one hard tear
torn from the eye of the inner
nostrils crying
no one howling at the moon.

There once was a wild perfume
floating with fingers grazing
and skin breathing all around
all around the air glazes with manna
taste the ground
die to hard boxes
inside ears, inside caves
pick through the rubble
clink and clatter on our tongues
tick
ticking
the man in the moon forgot his tune
ringing like crystal in the noon
of the sun
open our eyes, float on our backs
alphabet water talks to our spines
hello, hello
open our throats, spit each letter
into the blue
youu whooo, yyoouuu whhoooo
who can pull
the seed of a sound
from each blue
you are the who, we are the you

a stain of red presses into our spines
a piece of sky swims inside our mouths.

Mrs. Bigell's Garden

Open the eyes. Same room, stale air, fuzzy
red numbers in a box. Close the eyes, roll
to the other side, compact shoulder,
pull knees in tight. *Thoughts skip like*
stones across stagnant pools. Squeeze
the knees a little tighter. Walls are still
a muted beige. Ripples creep
toward the beige. Pull the covers around
the ball of shoulder. *Balls do not skip*
over water. Roll back to the other side.
Only flat stones are able to fly.

As a child of seven, I stand at the edge
of the yard peering through the fence
into Mrs. Bigell's garden, a magnificent
jungle of azaleas exploding in every color.
No wind, no chirping, no size to my body,
no catch in my throat, only pinks
and reds and yellows that spin
my eyes like flat suns across the yes,

roll on to the back. Stare at the ceiling.
Light is starting to lift above the level of see.
Stare at the walls. Beige has many variations.
Open the shoulders. Arch the back.
Stretch the arms into air,
no size, no wind, no sound.
Now, with the whole body,
yes, yes, yes,
rise!

The Next Trapeze

Late in the afternoon, the silence
of the boardroom is broken only
by the occasional squeak of a chair.

I am at the end of a dark tunnel
where passion lies like a dead fish
the ocean spat onto its shore,
an ominous reminder, one dulled eye
that stares at me in silent surrender.

I soar as a bright creature,
wings dusted with gold
to catch the sun and all the galaxies.
It is so easy, the way my fingers grasp
the bar of a gilded trapeze,
effortless the way my whole body
swings in magnificent arcs
that reach higher and higher,
until finally

I let go,
and there is nothing but my body and air,
suspended, motionless,
the next trapeze beyond my sight.

I float now in the silence of the room,
silent sounds lift me above dullness.
The one-eyed fish swims with me.
I wait for the next trapeze.

A Rope of Purple Light

I listen to you breathing in the next room,
hearts joined, our bodies still waiting.
It seems strange, both doors open
with nothing but our breath and the dim air
holding us apart. It is only moments
since long sobs fell from my chest
into the comforting forest of your arms.
Willow branches, these arms that sway with me
and around me. The delicate leaves of your fingers
feed me from roots growing deep within
the lake of glaciers and springs that speak no words.

I fall into the lake and for a moment decide to swim,
arms gliding through silver blue in continuous
curves that hold onto nothing, yet slice the vast cool
with the decisive pull of each arm. It isn't far to shore.
I lay my bare skin against a flat, broad rock,
honeycombed in the warmth of sun and granite.
For the first time, I know that the branches, the leaves,
the roots, the lake have always lived inside me.

Your breaths have settled into soft snores.
The purring of my cat stretches around my ears.
Air grows dimmer, a rope of purple light
appears, drifts across the hall and floats
between the rise and fall of our hearts.

Rice Paper Blinds

Holdreith

The pale light of early morning shimmers
through rice paper blinds,
a luminous form in yellow and rose
floating above our bodies entwined
in fresh sheets and soft flannel blanket.

I feel the delicacy of white paper
sift new life into this simple room
of one narrow bed that holds us together
like an empty page resting
between memory and imagining.

The darkness is growing thin, but
I can't quite touch the light, you say,
as the light washes over us filling
every dip and crack and space
that wants to be filled.

We rise from our bed and step into
the ordinariness of the day.
You cradle your coffee cup,
I butter crusty toast, the kettle whistles,
and light hums inside us, again.

Washed Glass

for Mike

I miss you in the blank sky of morning, silence
hovering above the hard crust on my plate.
A dull ache throbs behind my knees. My feet
are blocks of ice broken from a shining mass
that still floats in frigid waters.

When day is blue and light is white, I kneel
by the river, laying pieces of washed glass
on the grave. My breath catches with the cold
as the floating island crashes into frozen stacks
that rise like monuments on the shore.

I run my fingers along a smooth edge of glass,
remember hands carving leaded windows,
the smell of sandlewood lifting through the blue.
The glare of ice washes over me, leaves
a barely audible ring in my ears.

A mosaic of glass rests at my fingertips,
each piece shaped by the waters of its life.
I place the last piece into its empty space.
Light spills through the leaded windows.
Your scent dances in colors on the wall.

My Heart Returns to Paris

Holdreith

Devas, fairies, sprites of the wind and air
breathe inside the brick and mortar
of every *maison*, every *rue*,
breathe and whisper into sleeping eyes
and upturned lips of lovers,
heartstrings waiting to be stroked
with feathers of peacocks
and perfume of oils warmed in the sun.
Blessed amber of ancient queens pours
from their tongues. Like glistening threads
of jeweled tapestries, it weaves its way
into the quiet murmuring
of the heart.

Let me fly naked and shimmering
through the pale sky of my city's dawn.
Gentle rain washes my skin,
makes me holy as the moon.
Woo me, cathedraled city of love,
charm me, enthrall me till
I am drunken and captured in your spell.
Oh *Sacré Coeur*,
holy, holy, Hallowed Heart,
you are my beating and breathing,
my day and night.
Drink me in and pour me out,
silver light in the veins of life.
Drown me in your river of constant motion.
Hold me still and empty,
that I may know
every heart.

Garden Song

Golden petals wave like flags
atop the garden. Flies spiral
and leap from petal to leaf.
The silent beating of iridescent
wings is a song, if I listen.
Worms crawl like tiny snakes,
earth-crusted pink slides between
darkness and the sharp sparkle of day.
The sliding is a song, everything
is a sleepless song.

I kneel in garden prayer,
worm-pink of knees and feet
pressed into wet grass.
Fingers burrow, dirt
pushed tight under nails.
A baptism of earth and dew,
wet soil clings to my hands
pulling roots of feathered
weeds from their nest.

Staccato sounds bounce from a robin's
beak into warm air. Fat bees
grind their wings, the slow
buzzing of fingers moves in and out.
Dank earth. A barely visible
pulsing on the soft of my wrist.
The inner beating escapes.
I am the song

if I listen.

Prism

Dance inside the square box that lost its color.
Walls, once a deep red and lucid blue,
have slowly bleached
into layers of gray
that keep you in their spell.

Remove your dark glasses,
place them in a slot.
Lift the prism from where it was
forgotten many years ago.
Hold it to your eyes.
Fill the triangles of glass with voices that sing
in the key of weightless birds and holy diamonds.

In the sliver of the new moon, travel to the desert rock
that aligns with the perfect slant of the moon's shadow.
Dig with the soft of your fingers
into the broken shale and pulverized dust
until your hands are wet with all the colors.

Dance inside the box, walls exploding
into windows of a waking fountain,
feet branded, throat branded, eyes branded
with the brilliance of yellow that melts
the paste in your mouth and fills your lips
with the taste of flames bursting inside your heart.

Bury the box where the deepest strata of blue
begins to bleed into indigo.
Place the prism under your pillow and dream
about the village of people who speak
in the pulse of butterfly wings.

Lullaby

I
I lay myself down
I lay myself down to sleep,
beating the hammer
locked in the drum,
pound and pound
down and down.

Mother, Mother, hear my song,
I am a foghorn crooning
on the glass of a river black,
I am the first star
that falls tonight,
I am the core of the apple,
the teeth of the fatal bite.

I am an open mouth,
teach me how to wail.
I am eyes that are ears.
There is no place to hide.
I live in your guts
cause I've dug deep in mine,
and the beauty of guts
is they're all the same.
When you strain them
through the karma wheel,
they all tremble, break,
give up, give in,
wander helpless and alone.

II
Oh Mother, Mother,
Oh Father, Sister, Brother,
we're all little children,
with wide eyes staring
from under faces and masks

of days stretched so long
they fall off our bones
in a dull dry crack.

We sit up startled
in the abyss of night,
cold blue fright clanging.
Can you hear the whistle?
Can you hear the whistler blow, little babies?
Mamma's going to sing you a lullaby.
Hush now, hush now.
You forgot to cry.

Cry now babies.
The tears are your heart
starting to thaw.
Monsoons will baptize
your fortress of lack.
I am taking you back
to where you all began,
a formless form, nameless and bright,
pristine and floating in nothing but light.
Grow wings and fly above the fog,
breaking the barrier of every sound.
Hold what you've punished
in the feathered arms of your embrace.
This is your place, this is your song.

Sing now children
your own lullaby.
Love what you've hidden,
sleep deep and slow,
let the whistle blow,
pulling you into the sound of
hush,
hush,
hush.

Blackbird and White China

The bent sound of a blackbird sits
like a piece of cake on the windowsill.
Pads of fingers follow the neck.
Shoulders round, summer melons,
sumptuous orange painted on fading sheets.
Silver wings of tiny flies
hum at the window. Nestled.
Round saucer holds round cup.
Translucent white from delicate china
floats between fingers.
Chocolate crumbs dot the plate.
Flies hover under the ceiling,
speckled pins lighting the way.
Orange of summer melts on the plate.
We bend into the sound of blackbird.

John Morris

Eclipse of the Sun God

The loss of my wife to cancer, after forty-seven years of marriage, left me with a sense of emptiness that I didn't know how to handle. Not until one day when I was alone in an apartment in Woodstock, England, near the huge Blenheim Palace estate, while my family was off on holiday in Paris. After wandering for a time, I felt the urge to write. It had been many years since I'd even tried to write poetry—years during which my writing was limited to crabbed technical analysis designed for specialists. But that day, poem after poem appeared, as if by magic, in a yellow note pad. I felt alive again. I had somehow found the beginning of a new life, which is still unfolding before me.

The Loon

The loon is laughing in the lake,
diving, invisible,
then surfacing in some unexpected place
and laughing again.
Black and white,
he reflects the speckled surface of a life
that dives below
to come up laughing in the light.
The yin and yang that plunge
night into day and day into night.
The oruborus, the snake that eats its tail,
rolling like a child's hoop down the hill,
out of control, only to crash at the bottom,
like male and female, locked together
until that terrible rending
tears them apart.
But the laughing loon
does not want to be an allegory
and with a whoop goes back
to hide and seek.

The Star

White and shining Venus, burning bright,
pierces a hole in the velvet of night.
Lady of the waters
arise and bring me
your pure light.
In these shadowed streets
the stars themselves are hiding.

Candles

A candle flame has tiny sparks
riding in the golden pyramid,
a rainbow of colors, lemon yellow,
blue and white, with a bit of pumpkin,
rising proudly, casting light,
or sometimes fading to an ember,
a glowing spark, and then a wisp of smoke.

In the Night

In the night I heard the wind
blowing with your voice like the rustling leaves,
clear, chill, with only the moon watching
and only me listening:
I am with you always.
I am the air you breathe,
and I am within you and around you.
I am the fire burning with desire,
for I am the desired
and I am the lust that brings you to me,
for I am burning, burning,
reaching for the stars,
and I am the waters that quench the very
thirst that I have caused.
I am the question, and I am the answer.

You will find me as the earth beneath your feet,
firm, your strength in time of trial,
for I am your love, your only love,
bringing you warmth in the great night.

Roosevelt School

The merry-go-round on the playground
has frost on its blue-gray joints.
Frost has dusted the windows.
Trees are heavy and white.
White feathers on the bars
are marred with our fingerprints,
made with the fear
of fingers sticking to the frost,
sticking forever,
or at least until next spring.
Chains creak with each circle
and we grasp with thick gloves,
brown leather, padded,
a knit cuff holding them in place,
but now hopelessly stuck to the bar,
empty gloves hanging on for dear life,
ghost hands grasping for security,
no longer attached to arms,
a whirling world without their owner.
A splintering bench gives us a place to sit
in this tiny, spinning world
held by heavy links to its axis,
chains that bind us to a moving world
with our detached hands.
Below, in the playground's icy mud
there are tracks of other kids
whose lives went round in circles.
We can step in their footprints.

How to Brush Your Teeth

The goal is to find and extricate
each small bit, left over from dinner,
lunch, breakfast, snack, et cetera, caught
in the crannies of the mouth with its
white stalactites, stalagmites, reaching up
and down to masticate each bit
that you have eaten.
Your brush is like Hercules' tiny ship,
nearly caught, nearly crushed.
What carrots, celery, bits of creamy cake
have passed these gates into oblivion?
Your brush will free them,
restoring that brief time
of perfect cleanliness.
The sanitary brushing will absolve them
from all sin, from dirt,
from life's contamination.

Blenheim Palace

Poppies growing in a wheat field:
weeds are beautiful.
Black and white dogs bark frantically,
yin and yang in conflict, cooperating.
The half-moon wanes, watching the sun.
An ancient oak is still growing,
with leaves that pray like hands.
A white goose runs across the water,
wings flapping, feet barely touching.
Lichen, gold and silver patches,
on the old rocks.
A maze, yew hedges hiding the exit,
around and around, to another dead end.
Brilliant red butterflies rejoice
in their moment of life.
Not far off,
a white chalk horse is galloping
joyously.

Black Swans

This is the church
and this is the steeple.
Open the doors
and see all the people.
Open the doors to the cold wind of autumn.
Open the doors and see empty pews.
See stones in the churchyard,
covered with lichen.
See names inscribed for memory,
now unreadable.
Hear dogs barking
at the Stranger walking among them.
Hear the voice of the angry woman,
see the footpaths filled with strangers,
paths overgrown and impassable now.
Smell the wheat still green
under leaden skies,
with bright red poppies
at the edge of every field,
each red tongue licking the bees
in an orgy of pleasure.
The rabbits are black,
the swans are black,
the squirrels are black.
Monks hop, glide, leap,
each bearing the cloak of mourning.

Lasting Spring

The oak was eight feet across,
not dead, not yet, anyway.
A few green leaves clutched the sky.

I saw you dead, mouth agape,
no longer human.
The end had come,
leaving me with a thousand shattered
pieces of hope.
Papers, travel folders to places
we never visited,
a pile of natural health hints,
cures for cancer that didn't work.
Twenty-four large plastic bags
of notes, letters, ads,
unanswered, now never to be answered.
Eighteen photo albums,
vacations we dutifully took together.
Seventeen kinds of shampoo for your hair
that was never gray.
Clothing I finally sent off
to the Salvation Army,
saved for someone else.
Still in a drawer, carefully packed,
rarely used, our silver,
the lovely design we chose,
Lasting Spring.

Candlesticks for parties we never gave.
Outdoor furniture, citronella candles
to keep away bugs,
in case we ever had people over.
A TV set with a VCR that you bought
but never learned to use.
It was important to have one
on election night.
Your computer, an intricate labyrinth
that you somehow mastered.
One photograph with our daughter,
both of you laughing.
Precious copies of your book
and all the papers you gathered
for another book never written.
The wallpaper we both liked.
The drawers full of earrings.

If there is anything more empty
than our empty years together,
it is my empty life alone.

Hugs

I loved your body, warm,
pressed against mine.
Your breasts fit neatly into my chest.
Your lips were warm and full.
We were so close that every part of you
touched some part of me.
You brought me peace and joy.
You brought me love.

The second operation
left only two cruel red scars
where your breasts had been.
You wanted to hide the scars.
I could say only: Thank god you're alive.
It was as though the rottenness of others
brought rottenness to your body.
To go on endlessly fighting the dark.
To see honesty, the freedom from lies.

Night World

The night world is mystery.
A startled skunk has been foraging
under the bird feeders.
A raccoon wanders unperplexed
in a sudden floodlight.
One night when all were asleep
I heard a sudden scream,
perhaps of a mouse,
followed by the gentle whoo-whoo-whoo
of an owl, the night stalker.
Some nights in the woods,
you have to walk by feel, not by sight,
although, if you're lucky,
a rotting stump will be glowing
blue-green to light your way.

When the moon is void and the crickets silent
when the night leaves open no gaps of light,
when the earth has stopped,
when the owl drops silent on the fleeing vole
and ghosts make their filmy way among the trees,
when we are lost, terribly lost,
when no voice beckons us
and we stumble, fleeing the bat-winged monster,
when all is lost
and even death becomes a hope,
there in the forest gleams a light.

Hawks and Crows

I saw a hawk soaring high overhead
oblivious to the screaming crows,
whose warnings were the multitude
always afraid of strength and purpose.
Crows gather where they find a place to perch,
a common voice, in the excitement of the waning day.
The crows are said to return to the city
for the warmth they find in the presence of others.
A large tree can hold a thousand crows.
A hawk, on the other hand, will hunt alone,
perhaps in the company of one or two others.
The question that we all may ask,
as we watch them fly across the sky:
Is it better to fly in the company of a thousand others
or to soar alone, watching for the chance to dive,
silent, bringing sudden terror
to those that creep along the ground.

Butterflies

Hidden in the woods
tiny orange butterflies are dancing,
brown spots neatly symmetrical
accent their wings.
Sunlight through the leaves
makes them tiny jewels,
fragments of beauty, created for its own sake,
that I can see and take for my own.

To a Mouse

I found you this morning by the road,
victim of traffic, still perfect, intact,
with fur warm, brown,
for lining your tiny nest,
claws that could dig under the sod,
small teeth exposed, good for cracking seeds,
black beads for eyes that could see in the dark,
now blind, still, silent,
doomed to lie by the side of the road,
waiting for judgment day:
nothing sudden, no trumpets,
but the slow decay that faces all flesh.
Why, foolish mouse, were you out on the road?
Gathering seeds for babies,
now orphaned, starving, in the nest you built?
Or was it sheer joy,
the chance to dance in the moonlight,
a wild dance ending in the ecstasy of death?

Artichokes

An artichoke is, admittedly,
an acquired taste.
One must enjoy thick leaves.

Abrasives

Steel wool is good for cleaning pans.
Sandpaper smooths the edges of a board.
Sand upon the beach polishes the rocks.
A grindstone puts an edge on knives.
And so I remember your abrasive tone:
always ready to tear down my finest thoughts,
my carefully constructed interior castles,
all collapsed in flames and smoke.

Compost

Compost is shrugged-off leaves,
rubbery peels of oranges, rinds of melons,
rakings of the yard,
a few disintegrating paper napkins
now attended by a dancing troupe of tiny flies,
delicate connoisseurs of waste
whose taste devours this variegated pile,
life's striving to maintain itself.

Crows

Noisy arrogant gregarious
never an attempt at song,
they speak as unconscious alter egos
hidden in shadows,
a part of me that wants to scream
at the snowy owl in the woods.
The white ghost in the thicket
stirs us up in a chorus of cries
in the shadows of their ancient realm.

Eclipse of the Sun God

Lugh the Sun God looked at the sky
with a dull black hole
where the sun ought to be.
Still the sun's going down,
and Lugh the Sun God
looks at the sky,
into that black hole
where he dwells apart.
The empty nothing of the empty heart.

Amulets

A thousand of them
for our Gods and Goddesses.
Be with us, protect us,
bring us strength and healing.
Smite those who need smiting.
Bring me someone to love.
Help make dinner.
Bring us wealth
and the wisdom
to use it wisely.
Bring us joy:
a tiny dancing figure.
Bring us comfort,
a warm, embracing figure.
Let these amulets surround me.
May their power protect me.

Diana

Lovely moon, lady of the night,
pale white, gentle dreams,
skeleton trees, misty hills,
the hidden holes of rabbits,
lighting the world of the snowy owl,
she who watches and listens.
There is a kind of purity
unscratched by the light of day
when the Sun God's golden chariot
disappears from the realm of the sky.

Epiphany

You came to me in a swirl of color,
a rainbow reaching beyond the gray clouds,
to an unknown pot o' gold in my heart,
The sheer joyousness of Your presence
split through the clouds.

Green Man

The Green Man dwells in the forest,
a green globe of leaves, of grass,
of green fruit slowly ripening.
How do you like your forest home, Green Man?
Do you swing from tree to tree like a joyous monkey?
Do you hide, amused, as lowly humans hunt for you?
Do you eat bananas and carelessly drop the skins?
I wish I could live with you, Green Man.

The Elements

Air. Transparent.
Our link with life. Fragile as a pillow,
around and above, within.
Rattling the branches,
bringing disaster to an ancient oak,
blowing the skiff off-course.
Discoverer of forgotten islands.
Wild voice of the gale,
howling your threats at night.
Cool daughter of the storm,
bringer of fog,
invisible sustainer of kites.
Force of the unseen.

Fire's fingers reaching up.
Our mighty alchemist, maker of ashes.
Wild light, we see you in the night
as your hands grasp leaves,
shaking with the warmth of a deadly friendship.

Water. The thunder of the falls
stills to quiet all who watch
in the enforced silence of awe.
In the pool below a darting school of tiny minnows
is making endless circles, following the leader.
The morning dew has turned to frost,
and every tree is a crystal sculpture in the early sun.
Diamonds clatter to the ground.

The earth holds firm
beneath the fall of silver from the ancient sky.
Vast emptiness above and rock below.
All falls down to become one
with earth, the waiting mother.

Whenever you have need of anything
you will find it buried here.
Dig in the earth.
Find dreams, ashes left by ancient races,
bones turned to stone.

Late Winter

Deer tracks in the snow
along the path where rabbits run.
Patches of mud show the winter's thaw.

Joyce Harlukowicz

A Robin Startled from Her Sleep

Some time ago on a camping trip in the wilds of western Michigan, my friend prepared to retire to the cozy confines of her sleeping bag only to discover she was without her pillow. Since she grew up a city girl and was at a loss to solve her dilemma, I showed her how to take the sleeping bag stuff-sack, fill it with towels and socks, and Voila! Instant pillow.

As the oldest child, growing up with no siblings close in age and living in a rural area to boot, my independent, can-do, figure-it-out proclivity began early and persists to this day. I was a "late bloomer" with verbal skills, though I could see that the world was beautiful and drew it and painted it even in kindergarten. Then I learned to write. My first halting loops and lines gave way to flowing cursive strokes. Words and ideas so slow to materialize on my tongue soon spilled onto the page.

I learned that you write to other people—and when they write back, you can feel their voice, the caress of their presence, their very essence in the marks on the page. Letters from my dearest uncle in Pennsylvania, on paper from the dimestore in Bridgeville, all had a peculiar loop on the "y" when he wrote "Cuddy, Penna." I discovered, next to the bottle of peppermint schnapps, my mother's perfect, champion penmanship in her personal drawer where she kept rhymed poetry hidden from those she loved. My father's careful, large, eighth-grade educated strokes appeared on cheap

notecards ordered from catalogs, newsprint images of his beloved
antique trucks which, he figured, were my favorite, too. Growing up
poor, we were always fixing up some tired and nearly worn-out truck
so he had a way to get to his laborer's job. When I was his constant
and curious sidekick, few words passed between us, but I learned
how to gap a spark plug and deftly replace all the needle-like
bearings in a four-post U-Joint, things his large fingers fumbled. The
cards began arriving in the years after I'd left home, telling me
things of the heart that he couldn't say aloud.

Robert Frost once said that writing was for him "a momentary stay
against confusion." Writing for me is an abiding and life-sustaining
oasis, my words the stroke of an unseen hand as I, like my father,
write about things which couldn't be said aloud. It is much like my
uncle's simple summation, uttered with satisfaction when once again
on the hillside farm we found a way to fix-up and make-do: if you
live long enough, you find enough pillows.

Sleepless on June 21

Before the dawn, folding clothes.
At the end of a load, one sock, inexplicably,
turned inside out.

At the end of the lane, on the highway,
an explosion. A robin startled from her sleep
sings instantly.

Last night at dinner, the hand on the back,
the elusive endearments, a transient gaze.
When did tears turn to dust?
Like stiletto heels on a hardwood floor,
round, resonant, hollow with the soft edge
of age, the tongue and groove of ennui.

Doing a light load, folding the underwear.
In the pith of years when the circle of arms
turns to dust in the shoes,
the lovers walk out and the living runs on,
life is just a jester who's been surprised.

We smile, politely, to hide the hollow
of emptiness. Aside the swift and flowing
surface, the hellebores are blooming
by the second pond.

Mother and Daughter

Harlukowicz

Mother, from the edge of your grave,
do you wonder about your daughter?
I pass by those roadside shrines, hear hymns
across shaven Midwestern fields on a fall afternoon
of long, tired light, our seasons in transition—

in your image a daughter, who learned early to wear
the uniforms of our culture. Mother: once the semblance
of refuge, now the ghost of hope that often fails. Still
no one can tell me why cartoon characters wear white gloves,
why some lovers stay longer than others,

or why pain runs as a deep river swept by autumn fires
and you became not someone I loved but only someone I knew.
Mother, do you place your gaze with judgement,
lament these trials, and at last, abandon kinship?

How I long again for that day on that steep walk, up
from the Oregon coast, when you put your hand in my pocket
and laced your fingers around mine.

Ode to Elijah

And what is your life
        but the harvest of wisdom glazed
        by a winter storm on the first day of spring?

Ice thunders through the branches and piles
        in drifts in the tulip beds.

Long ago you walked from Three Mile to Eight Mile,
        the snow a silken overcoat,
        but the job was gone.

The little ones saw you mount the steps
        in the crystalline glow of the gaslight.

I want to ask: did you know love?
        and what was it like; was it
        real then?

But it is nothing now, the arms fall dormant,
        the embrace a deserted stare,
        what was then is not now, ever.

Like the echoes of a train-whistle off the walls
        of the river valley, it passes
        through us, and we know.

You ask how I know this affair, the poignant panoply
        that nothing falls without knowledge.

The dead sparrow hears a requiem.
        I say it rings like the sun off Wolcott Mill Pond
        where the children stuff their pockets with frogs.

A Conversation with Clovis

There is that odd play of light in your words,
the smallest glide toward knowing,
the reach of communion, beyond the dark hide
of loneliness. But it passes as if we were ghosts,
drawing back into that Sunday morning pocket
where you rest on the weathered step by the back door.

And what are words but scavengers we send
to ponder the possible, culling through the calamity of living,
separating truth and lies like the roadside raven
sifts serendipitous offerings?
He arises, and wheels slowly, slowly, overhead.

The late winter sun's rays flood through the railing
on the deck, leaving a pattern of light, dark, light, dark
on the veil of our utterance. I connect the long gray shadows
spilling on the snow with the warmth of my hand.
The raven looks beyond the lines, and sees.

First Blizzard

The wind pummels windows, pitching
soft-shelled kernels of ice against the gable.
Drifts shape soft crescents around the spruces
where some small creature will spend the night.

I close my eyes and remember when your presence
filled this room, your comfort
shutting out cacophony, the wild swinging branches of bitterness
not much more than distant sighs.
The wind turns corners and rattles the door.

For now, most things bow down, in this snow,
from this storm. And I miss you: I can't tell
where the grass ends
and the sidewalk begins.

Harlukowicz

Let Morning Come

with thanks to Jane Kenyon's "Let Evening Come"

Night lingers on tender threads
braced to the wings of clouds.
Let morning's doves draw back its covers
on a murmur liquid like the soft blue
of the horizon line.

The wind finds its words on cattails by the stream.
Dark is broken underfoot; the sky lays hands
of luminescent mists on the sedges by the shore.
Let morning come.

The edges of the clouds evanesce from somewhere deep,
drift upward from the cool east to the rim
of the lower west. Like Cimmerian° flocks racing above,
they eclipse the great shining faces overhead.
The evening star doesn't know where to hide.
Let morning come.

Night creatures resist no more,
and give themselves back to the darkness.
Gentle rises the day,
the world its audience.
Let morning come.

° *The Cimmerians were a mythical people, described by Homer as dwelling in a
remote land of mist and gloom.*

Four Hours to Kalamazoo

The maple on Dequindre Road loses its summer life,
leaf by leaf. Sometimes dawn shines through
in unexpected places; sky-holes flicker in the morning mists
on the floodplain. Crows row deep black strokes
above the gloaming, casting sharp, furtive glances, no carrion below.

Little by little that tree surrounds itself
with a brazen autumnal lover's blush.
Like a crescent moon that gives way
to the seasoned fullness of the eclipse,
each day that blush overtakes
the blue-green heat of August.
Thousands pass by, headlights blazing,
innocent of knowing.

It's four hours to Kalamazoo; my words abide
in your crystal bowl on the nightstand.
The toaster is hardly cold in Elmira,
where lights in the farmhouse blaze brighter
than the dawn. Like heat from a comet's tail,
I shrug them off into the black aurora
of the western sky. I move my life forward
between the lines: yellow line left, white line right.

Uncle's Legacy

The trash man from Pittsburgh collected used pots and pans.
You can make good money, he said. Copper and brass
gleamed funny, dented little smiles, the cast iron heavy
and sullied with rust. It seared my small hands
in the noonday heat on the hilltop,

where we pitched them to piles like hilltop haystacks.
We hauled away those pots to the dump by the quarry
and money changed hands. To a ten-year-old's eyes,
flowers and lace danced with money in the window
at Mooney's in Bridgeville. Uncle's hand was heavy in mine
as we strode next door to the shoe store,

brass eyelets like sentries on the new boots. Delicate brass buckles
adorned white pumps; but Uncle wanted hilltop tough
tramping shoes, orange leather and thick, heavy soles with ridges,
shoes like the boys wear, to kick pots and footballs and playground
bullies. No thought of money for sleek satin collars,
like the ones on girls he held hands with,

when they smiled into each other's eyes,
hands around the waist pulling each other close
to the brass buttons on his double-breasted flannel
suit, the best money could buy. I saw those old pictures,
snapped outside the hilltop home, edges faded, curled,
kept in the cookbook by the pots near the stove.
On days when Mother's heart was heavy

I sometimes caught her leaning, heavy on the counter,
her eyes gleaming, shining as her hands cradled years
distant, while tears leapt, reflected in the pots
that shone like the years, music from brass bands
and big-time orchestras like hazy hilltop mornings.
When the quarry folded, no one had money for fine things

and dances, and some fled to make money in the Motor City.
Those who stayed had not money nor love, hearts heavy
as the valley mists, confined to days in labor on hilltop farms
and nights in the valleys of loneliness. Time marched away
from Uncle, but for me brazen mornings on tranquil
hilltops bridge the span like pots to the hands,

a summons to the hilltop of memory which money cannot buy.
When winds heavy and dark glow like brass,
his grace cradles my hands.

At Dawn Three Blackbirds

sit like sentinels
at the top of the tree just over the hill.
      A red-orange blush tinges the fine branches
      clothed with March hoarfrost.

I pass by, looking for days
of simple truths and inalienable rights.
      Highway marquees of bible verse jostle
      with the drive-in's salacious offerings.

A large truck gives way in a syncopated dance,
and I glide gracefully into the northbound lane.
      It's a long way from the time we walked on water
      in our mother's womb,
      to living with a man from San Diego.

A broken door lies by the side of the road.
Gone are the sunrises from which symphonies are written,
      where we pay for our art
      with the vexation of living.

Three blackbirds sit on a sign, berobed,
to protest a grave injustice: eighty acres for sale.
      Two lanes will become four, and the last man
      in a long familial line will become rich, for a time.

World, I am your slow sojourner, dispirited muse,
a soul formed at some unavoidable silent explosion.
      Nothing's certain, except for charred toast, coffee,
      and three blackbirds greeting the dawn.

Giving Away the Farm

In the last year of his life he confided this to me,
while we stood in the old orchard.
The boy doesn't want it, so I'm going to give it to the girl.

The sun wriggled through layers of flannel, long fingers
of the last warmth of late autumn.
The air hung close with the brown ripe fetor
of the early apples left on the branches.

The deer will feed on the windfall.
The daughter will dower these aged trees,
these sheds, the spring that runs without reason.

No matter, he said about the pipeline that runs deep
under the land, at the odd angle, on the other side of the road.
The son knew about that.

It took a lot; he imagined the boy might come to know one day.
The girl could wait for the royalty checks; she'd know.
But it's for the son that doors are never latched.
As long as the last ember is in the stove, the draft never closes.

One does not query why some sing, some recite,
some turn night into day.
For a time we rejoiced, looked back,
said, *What a good time was had by all.*

She took the best of this promised land, gathered up
like winesap still good enough for pie. Some good pie will
quiet the body before bed.

I watched her shape the dough, rolled just so thin, ridges pinched
along the edge. Cold spring water makes the crust crisp.

The embers in the firebox flared; the oven gauge leapt toward hot.

Cages

The morning moon clings to the western sky.
Outside, the portulaca struggle to bloom.
Doves fill their languished maws from small tepid pools.

At the corner of Pekins Road, a man stands with a shopping cart.
He speaks soundless words to a lemon-gold finch
imprisoned in a fragile wire cage. In the small morning light
the bird sings, scattering liquid pieces of dawn.

I live like a bird in a cage,
my mind an empty womb, a noble ruin
which rakes the coals of memory.

Sleeping with the homeless in the streets of Paris,
old roses twine the wrought iron railing. Lilies wash
their heady essence over me, mingled with
sharp yeast rising from the bakery below.

Lies

Wearied by the warmth, you toss unrecognizable syllables
in your predawn sleep. A sudden chill of air through the screen.
The treads of my rocker carve silent, even wedges of darkness.

Sometimes things look good and right to our eyes:
lies told as a twilight of truth, the singing we once heard
as one, the clock forever stopped at thirteen past eleven.

An airplane drones overhead, pauses, and drones onward
through the upper end of day, into the far-reaching
shadow that gives meaning to sweet hours of sleep.

On the Back Porch in Plastic Chairs

The glass of tea you hand me
has no mint leaves in it, and I wonder
if you've lost your southern manners

as we lost our innocence, not one summer
but many, while our lives grew like orbits
beyond the gravel road with a landfill on it,
past where Nine Mile turns to dirt, until we thought
we were past the exact measure of the judging universe.

Through the one tall, slender poplar in the yard
the moon dusts its glassine light on geese
feeding on the beveled plain by the pond.
Sweet hypnotic tones of cicadas pause,
while moonlight admires the peony
by the railing of the porch, shining
silver-white, taut, round, and full.

Remember the road trip through the Plains
in a used Buick Skylark, one of us a pilgrim,
the other a tour guide? Standing by the faith,
I reckon you are guilty of far more grace than I,
content to admire things from afar.

Patricia Washburn

Dancing on the Precipice

A strange thing happened to me a few years ago. My life disappeared. To be more specific, I suddenly couldn't think of any earthly reason for my existence. I had become superfluous, *persona non grata*. It happened this way.

Early one June, my mother expressed the desire to move "closer to family." It seemed that no one in the city of Chicago cared whether my parents lived or died. The following week, my father fell and broke his arm. He was sent to a nursing home for physical therapy. I began the daunting task of packing their accumulated household goods of sixty-three years together. By late August, we were ready for the movers. That was when my father's condition worsened. He died a few days later. We made the decision to carry on with our plans, though my mother was noticeably confused. All of her belongings were on the moving van, except for the clothes she wore and the small box containing my father's ashes. Without him, in unfamiliar surroundings, my mother seemed disoriented and needy. She desperately wanted her old life back, but the life she remembered so fondly had taken place years earlier. It included a healthy husband and no hint of dementia. She had already forgotten that moving had been her idea. The enormity of the responsibility I'd taken on began to sink in.

The following spring, I came down with a painful and debilitating case of shingles. Three weeks later, and no better, I was diagnosed with mononucleosis. I felt old, depleted, and used up. Anxiety attacks and claustrophobia plagued me. Enclosed places, like airplanes, buses, even movie theaters made me feel panicky. I couldn't sleep without a nightlight. Listlessly, I moved through the motions of daily life as well as I could. I both loved and hated my mother, and felt tremendously conflicted about it. Incredibly, my father's death had been my first close encounter with mortality. Now my mother was deteriorating badly, and I was overcome with profound sadness for both of us. Somehow it felt as if my life were over, too. I was convinced I had squandered it with endless procrastination.

One day I happened across Julia Cameron's book, *The Artist's Way*. Designed to help reach the innermost places of our minds, things we don't even know exist, the book soon became my lifeline. Cameron's most elemental rule is to keep a journal. Write three pages, longhand, every day, anything that comes into your head. I'd always considered myself a writer, but my writing habits were lackadaisical and haphazard at best. I went to the drugstore and bought a beige notebook, a jumbo pack of lined paper and a rollerball pen. It was the most positive thing I'd done for myself in a long time. I was grateful for any sense of direction and excited to begin. Next morning I sat at my desk and stared into my coffee cup, blank notebook in front of me. I tried to write, one halting word at a time, but I couldn't fill up one page. After an hour, I gave it up for the day. Had I put it off too long? Perhaps any gift I'd had was gone. Disheartened, I went back to the beginning of Cameron's book and read again the purpose of the three pages. The next morning I went back to my desk, and the next.

Gradually, the journal began to be the reason I got up every morning. It became my ritual: the coffee, the rolltop desk, my pen, my notebook. Very slowly, the words began to flow. I saw how blocked I'd become, how much I'd stored away unexamined. I learned that I was like a ticking time bomb. The pages in those early days were full of anger. I wrote about guilt and insecurity, fear and frustration, and crushing fatigue. I raged at my mother for the relationship we'd never had and for the shambles she'd made of my life. I screamed out loud on the page. The sky didn't fall. My journal became my most trusted ally, always there for me, impartial and non-judgmental. The more I wrote, the more I wanted to write. The more I got onto the page, the better I felt.

I started to write about my mother's death, though it was still months away. In a sense, I had been grieving for her all along. Unresolved issues littered our past like a minefield; I'd have to work through them by myself. But I began to understand that I had been a pretty good daughter—at least I'd done my best—and I had to admit that the same needed to be said of my mother. I stunned my family by buying a navy blue suit to wear at her funeral, though she was technically still alive. I felt the end was near. This time I was prepared for it. She died in April.

On Mother's Day, we held a memorial service for my parents and planted a tree over their mingled ashes. When the pastor read the lovely words from Ecclesiastes: "For everything there is a season, and a time for every purpose under heaven . . . ." my heart leaped. It had been nearly two years since my father's death and the beginning of my mother's decline, nearly two years of mourning for them both. It was enough. I gave myself permission, finally, to set about the business of my own life. The time to mourn was past. It was a new day, a time to dance.

His Name Was Jimmy

When he fell into the icy lake, did he
think, just for a moment, he'd get a
spanking when he got home, for ruining
his shoes? Did he have his mittens on?
Was he wearing snow pants and boots?
Did he cry out for his mother?
Second-graders wonder about these things.
Did he open his eyes under the water? I
never could do that. Did his glasses
stay on his face, or did they fall away,
drifting down slowly through
Lake Michigan's thick, winter water,
coming to rest near his small body?

On my way home at lunchtime, I passed two
Chicago policemen, talking on the corner.
Hear anything about the kid? one asked.
The other made a fist and turned his
thumb down. My mother wanted to know if
I'd heard anything about my teacher's
little boy. I showed her what the
policeman did with his thumb.
Oh, my mother said, so flat and final,
I knew he must be dead.
His name was Jimmy.

My teacher wasn't there in the afternoon.
Someone else taught my class for the
longest time. It was spring when she
came back to school. She looked so
different to me. I think I'd almost
forgotten her by then. But that boy
is like my own child now. He's been with me
all these years, safe and warm
under soft, blue blankets, sound asleep.

Goddess of the Vineyard

Upon the chimney wall outside my door, amid the tangled ivy vines, there lives a goddess. Clusters of lush grapes surround her winsome features: imposing brow, majestic nose, sculpted lips, all encircled by a grapevine wreath. Her dreamy gaze attends some far horizon. *The Goddess of the Vineyard* is her name, though in truth, there are no fields of grapes nearby.

Her expression doesn't change when streaked with rain, when rivulets crisscross her face and heavy droplets fall from the tip of her nose and chin, or when snow adorns her hair and gathers at the corners of her eyes. No stinging sleet or bitter wind prevails against her peaceful countenance. She is impervious to nature, for the most part—except when the spinner comes.

Unlikeliest of friends they are, the goddess and the spinner, stealthy as children up past their bedtimes, mischievous and giddy. The spinner comes in dark of night when all is still and by moonglow begins his work: a shimmering crown, perhaps, to dress her hair, enticing gossamer mask to hide her eyes, or bridal veil, ethereal and demure. The spinner weaves his magic through the night.

At daybreak he departs. I think of him just out of sight, stifling giggles and clutching his many legs to himself, as I survey his wondrous handiwork, the iridescent threads encrusted now with diamonds in pale morning light. Thus arrayed, the goddess keeps her vigil at the chimney wall. Upon her face I think I see the most illusory of smiles, so enchanted is she, still, by the visit of the spinner.

Sudsing Tom Selleck

I dream I am in the shower with Tom Selleck. The real Tom Selleck. It is somewhere in Hawaii, the big island. Not just a regular shower, but a tiled, tropical rain forest with hot and cold running water. We are trapped there, locked in by the bad guys, or something. It is only a matter of time before the authorities come to rescue us.

Meanwhile, Tom is even more gorgeous up close than I ever imagined: dimples and mustache, glistening tan body, rippling muscles, tight white buns, chest hair . . . all the way down. Oh, God!

In the shower with Tom Selleck. A little sudsing, a little schmoozing, a lot of laughing. We're comfortable with each other, Tom and I, familiar as if we'd been together forever. We communicate in that lazy, wordless way people do in dreams, drifting. Suddenly, I hear a word, hear it distinctly, a word I don't expect to hear— " . . . resistible."

"Huh?" I'm paying attention now.

He laughs. "I said I find you resistible." As God is my witness, that is what the man says to me. I'm resistible. Well, thank you very much!

"Resistible," I say. "Whaddyamean, resistible? This is my dream, goddammit! You can't find me resistible."

He puts his warm hands on my shoulders. "Look," he says, "I really like you. You're a lot of fun. I mean, jeez, what can I say?" The kiss-off from Tom Selleck in my own dream.

"I don't understand," I whimper. "What can I do? Anything. Name it. Tom?" No answer.

Sleep experts believe it is possible to become pro-active in our dreams. With practice, they say, we can learn to select the subject of our dream and fine-tune the outcome to our satisfaction. Once mastered, this skill is said to lead to a more successful, take-charge life. To this, I say, Baloney! Never, in the history of the world, has a woman tried so hard to re-dream a dream.

Suddenly, I notice daylight through my eyelids, just as I hear the announcer say, "Ladies and gentlemen, Tom Selleck has left the building."

Crosswind

for my father, Ralph Maheu Borden

"Would you like a few minutes alone with him?" the director asked. It was the last thing Sarah Ballentine wanted.

"Yes, thank you." She forced a smile. When the call had come, she'd made the drive from Detroit to Chicago in four and a half hours. Now she noticed that her sweat pants and tee shirt were out of place here.

The director escorted her to a large, immaculate room. "Take all the time you need."

On a table at the far end of the room lay the body of Sarah's father, Randall Jenner. It was to be cremated according to his wishes, whenever the medical examiner came and signed the papers. Sarah breathed deeply, trying to shake off the road. This wasn't supposed to happen. He wasn't supposed to die.

For the past few weeks, Sarah had received mixed messages. The doctor at Brentwood Nursing Home had called just that morning and spoken encouragingly of her father's improved vital signs, good color, and progress in physical therapy. But to Sarah's mind, her father didn't have the look of a man on the mend. Lately, he'd been obsessed with the notion of escape. He'd mentioned it every time she'd visited. He believed himself to be a prisoner at Brentwood. Now Sarah understood that her father had been talking about death. She could guess that one of his last thoughts might have been, "I'll show the bastards!"

Cremation was a decision he'd clung to when he'd forgotten nearly everything else. Sarah wondered if he'd remembered her at the last. He'd squint at her, agitated, his faded blue eyes long ravaged by macular degeneration. It was when he heard her voice that a glimmer of recognition lit his face. "Oh, I know you!" he'd say, pleased with himself.

He'd been so cold these past few months, ever since the fall that broke his arm and sent him to Brentwood for rehabilitation. Sarah thought of flames warming his body before consuming it for all time. Could hell be much different? she wondered. Sarah preferred to imagine him dozing by a crackling fire, afghan over his knees, large-print *Reader's Digest* open on his lap. Sarah knew she had an amazing capacity for avoidance. She'd managed to steer clear of the issue of her own mortality until now.

She advanced to the narrow table where her father lay, his small body draped in white cloth. He had stood six feet tall in his manhood. Sarah liked to remember him that way, before osteoporosis had begun to steal from him, a quarter-inch at a time. How handsome he looked now, his face smooth and untroubled, far beyond the indignities of Brentwood. She bent and kissed his cold forehead.

At the memorial service, Sarah told some stories about her father. It had been customary for Randall to read his daughter a bedtime story every evening. *The Ugly Duckling* had captivated her imagination. She'd wanted to hear it again and again. Sarah had watched when her father began a new oil painting. He didn't tolerate unnecessary conversation, nor was it uncommon for him to fling sable paintbrushes across the room or kick the radiator when the work wasn't going well. Sarah's mother would call out from the kitchen, "Now, Randall, calm yourself." When she overheard him saying naughty words, which he often did, she'd scold him. "Randall, please! Little pitchers have big ears, you know." Sarah thought that was funny.

To Sarah's delight, a pair of majestic white swans had come to life on the canvas. They were gliding, side by side, on indigo blue water. The painting was a birthday present for Sarah, who considered it the most beautiful thing her father had ever painted. She'd called him an artist. "I'm no artist, Sarah," he'd said, chuckling.

"Then what are you, Daddy?" she'd asked, puzzled.

"Just a guy who likes to paint pictures."

Randall had often painted a solitary figure somewhere in his landscapes. Long ago, Sarah had come to believe the figure was himself—for he was a loner, a solitary man, and wary of his fellow man. He used to say, "Don't fall down, or the pack will tear you to pieces." One afternoon at Brentwood, Sarah had offered to cut her father's long fingernails. In a trusting, almost childlike gesture, he'd held out his bruised and swollen hand in its dirty, elbow-length cast, and allowed her to give aid and comfort. It was one of her tenderest memories of him, and there was no explaining why.

A season of interminable heat followed the funeral. Temperatures hovered near one hundred degrees for weeks, with no relief in sight. The air was so thick and close, it was hard to distinguish inhaling from exhaling. Sarah watched as dazed birds splashed in the steamy birdbath, then hung their wings out like laundry on a line, hoping for a whisper of a breeze. She kept herself busy with her father's affairs: filling out paperwork, mailing copies of the death certificate, disposing of his personal effects. Some of his paintings had to be crated and sent to the relatives who had spoken for them.

Daytime was easier for Sarah. It was far into the night when flames danced before her eyes, or the dream came again, and she embarked on another futile search for the box of her father's ashes. She had even become a little claustrophobic, at this late stage of the game.

It was unusually quiet on Crosswinds Boulevard for a summer Saturday afternoon. Sarah noticed that the lawn had been cut while she was out grocery shopping. She spotted one perfect red and gold maple leaf on the velvety grass. Odd for leaves to be turning this early, she thought. Sarah brought the groceries in and set them on the counter. She glanced out the kitchen window and noticed a hummingbird hovering over the hanging basket of flowers, the whir of its tiny wings audible through the screen. Sarah stood, spellbound, until it veered out of sight. The eerie call of a cicada pierced the still summer air, rising sharply like a tea kettle at the boil, then falling away to nothing. The sound continued to reverberate against Sarah's eardrums. Everything felt peculiarly intense, colors and sounds magnified. A shiver snaked its way up Sarah's spine. She experienced a feeling of time warp, a sense of imminent portent. Then Sarah felt herself surrounded by light. Tranquility washed over her, flooding her awareness.

Sarah smiled. She realized in that moment that her father was exactly where he belonged. He was all right.

Monday's child is fair of face,
Tuesday's child is full of grace,
Wednesday's child is full of woe,
Thursday's child has far to go,
Friday's child is loving and giving,
Saturday's child works hard for a living,
But the child that is born on the Sabbath day,
Is bonny and blithe and good and gay.

Thursday's Children

We have always known each other, Roseanna and I. Long before we drew our first breath, looked into our mother's eyes, or felt the sunshine on our faces, we'd bonded for all time. Like tadpoles jumping and diving in a dim pool, aware of each other's presence every hour of the day and night, we communicated from our earliest moments. We were identical twin sisters, Hanna Rose and Roseanna Lynn Brandt, born under Gemini, the sign of the twins, Castor and Pollux. I was the first-born, and always had a sense that I was the stronger sister.

Sometimes I think that twins are as misunderstood as cats. There is folklore about us that passes for knowledge. I've heard it said that twins can read each other's minds. Well, yes and no. There comes a time when that gift of childhood intuition fades away, often just when it's needed most.

We lived in a small apartment in Chicago with our parents, Jack and Dorothy Brandt. Our father was a great storyteller and game-player who always had time to work puzzles with us, play hide-and-seek, and read to us every bedtime. He hardly ever missed an evening. I still remember his wonderful smile, the sound of his laugh, and the smell of his after-shave, and most especially, the giddy feel of being swooped up and held high over his head. That is how I choose to remember my father.

By the time Roseanna and I were in first grade, our family was on a steep economic downturn. It seemed that for all his endearing qualities, our father didn't have the knack of holding down a job. He was perpetually in search of the perfect opportunity. To the best of anyone's knowledge, he never found it. He and Mama began to spend long evenings at the kitchen table discussing their worsening financial situation and the unavoidable wrath of our grandfather when he found out about it.

Ben Smith, our grandpa, always said he was a "self-made man." Whatever he put his mind and muscle to made money for him. And Benjamin Franklin Smith never spent a wrong dollar, either. He and our grandma, Margaret, lived a comfortable if understated life. Grandpa couldn't tolerate a man who didn't provide well for his family, particularly where Grandpa's only child, Dorothy, was concerned. Grandpa began helping out financially, as he felt obliged to do. Unfortunately, his opinions came right along with his money. God knows, he had plenty of both.

One evening, we overheard our grandparents arguing. "Margaret, I don't know why you refuse to see what's as plain as the nose on your face. The man is irresponsible, I tell you." We knew instantly who Grandpa was talking about. Grandma spoke quietly, as if to calm Grandpa down. He snarled back at her, merciless as a dog with a ham hock. "Don't you 'Now, Ben' me, Margaret! The man doesn't even have a job. They don't have a pot to piss in or a window to throw it out of." We noticed that Grandpa called our father "the man" instead of Jack. "Jesus H. Christ, Margaret, think about Dorothy. And what about those little girls, hmm? What about Hanna and Roseanna? Don't you think they deserve a chance? Who is going to provide for their futures? Just answer me that, Margaret." But Grandma didn't answer.

We spent most of that summer at our grandparents' home on Greenwood Street. Our father visited only once during that time. To us, he seemed an altogether different man. In the presence of Ben Smith he looked smaller, less sure of himself. I think Grandpa could smell fear, and when he did, he moved in for the kill. By September, Mama had brought all of our belongings to the Greenwood house. There was going to be a trial separation, she told us, and that was that. End of discussion. I noticed for the first time that Mama could make her mouth into a long, thin, straight line across her face just like Grandma could.

Our happiest times were the summers up north at Grandpa's cottage on Comfort Lake. It was a child-dominated retreat. Women dutifully cleaned fish, picked up after children and spouses, saw to the shopping, swept up sand, and were responsible for just about everything, freeing the dads and granddads to the pursuit of pleasure for whatever precious little time they had there, often just long weekends. For us, though, it was the whole glorious summer, from the end of June until almost Labor Day. Rosie and I stayed in our bathing suits all day long. We were always on the beach or in the water with kids from the neighboring cottages. Grandpa's boats were reputed to be the fastest ones on the lake. The first thing we would do, Rosie and I, while Mama and Grandma aired out the cottage and took the sheets off the furniture, was go into the woods and gather huge armloads of purple and white lilacs, enough to fill every corner of the cottage with their fragrant beauty. Whenever I think of the cottage, I smell lilacs.

We were allowed to eat things at the cottage that we never had at home, things like smoked fish, beef jerky, and honey in the comb, and sometimes we even had 7-Up with dinner instead of milk. Mama and Grandma baked fruit pies while Rosie and I took turns cranking the ice cream freezer out on the porch. Every evening after dark, people gathered on the beach for a bonfire, and there were always marshmallows to roast.

The safest I ever felt was in that cottage late at night when Grandpa and his friends were downstairs playing cards, the rich aromatic smoke from his Havana cigars wafting up to the loft where Rosie and I were presumed to be asleep. The sounds of their banter and good-natured cussing, and the clatter of poker chips on the kitchen table filled me with a sense of well-being. In that time and place, surely no harm could befall us.

Our father, from whom we were now officially divorced, sent us an envelope on the first of every month. It bore no return address and contained no message—nothing at all except bill-sized slips of plain green paper.

○   ○   ○

Mama's choice for a second husband took us by surprise. So different was he from our father, he might as well have come from another planet. He was much older than Mama, for one thing, and already married for another. And there was the matter of the money. Warren Shepherd was a bona fide millionaire. He was a tall, thin, bow-legged man, rangy looking like an old cowboy. He had wooly gray hair and a nice gap-toothed smile. He also had, Rosie and I thought, a serious attachment to one Jack Daniel's.

The first time we met Warren, he was sitting on the piano bench, back to the keys, bottle in one hand, glass in the other. "How do you do?" he asked, his head bobbing back and forth comically between Rosie and me. Wisely, Mama had cautioned us ahead of time to be on our best behavior. "I make it a policy never to drink before noon," he confided, checking his watch. It was five minutes to twelve. "Well, maybe just this once," he winked at us as he poured.

At first, Rosie and I thought Warren was just a big blowhard, but it turned out we were wrong. He was smart and funny, generous as anything, and completely devoted to Mama. That was good enough for us. One glance at Warren's bankbook was all it took for Grandpa to give his stamp of approval.

When Warren's divorce became final a few months later, he married our mother and took her to California. It was a foregone conclusion that Rosie and I would stay with our grandparents, Mama being on her honeymoon and all. And just that quickly, our status changed, more dramatically and with more finality than either of us could have comprehended. When our mother married Warren, we reconciled ourselves to it in a theoretical sense, but it effectively removed her from our lives. We hadn't fully understood that part. Now we were children once removed, guests in our grandparents' home, as good as they were to us. This was a time I think of as our half-life, almost a time of suspended animation. We bargained endlessly with each other and any higher power we thought might listen to kids. If we stop being bratty to Grandma, Daddy will call. If we make our beds and clean our room every single day, Mama will come back for us. If we get straight A's on our report cards, Mama and Daddy will get married again.

When we visited Mama and Warren in Sausalito we felt like guests there, too. Mama fussed over us, acting like she always did when company came, not like a person does with her own children. She asked what we were studying in school and who our friends

were. Our own mother didn't have a clue about us. Rosie and I
didn't belong there. We didn't know where we belonged anymore.
When the visit was over, we returned to Chicago and our
grandparents, our naive, little-girl dreams sinking further out of sight
with every passing day.

○   ○   ○

Cheerleaders and drum majorettes were the "innies" at Rogers
Park High School. They were friends with each other and with the
teams: the football, basketball, and baseball players, and the
swimmers, all of whom were automatically "innies." Brainy kids
hung out with other brains. Goody-goods stuck together, and so did
the Rotcee boys and the hoods. Then there were the "outties," who
didn't belong to any particular group but were friendly with "innie"
kids as well as their "outtie" friends. That was Rosie and me

Grandma made us formal dresses for our senior prom. Mine was a
strapless black taffeta with a black tulle overskirt. I wanted to look
sophisticated. Grandma didn't approve of strapless dresses, or black
for that matter, on young girls, but she gave in this once.

When the band took their first break of the evening, we went out
on the veranda. There was a nice breeze off the lake. The air felt
fresh and cool. Suddenly, Jim Grafton, star quarterback of the
football team, appeared next to me. He put his sweaty hand on the
back of my neck. "Having a good time, Hanna?" he asked. Before I
could answer, he said, "I never noticed how pretty your mouth is.
God, there's an aura around your lips. I swear it! I want to kiss you,"
he whispered. My heart pounded in my ears as he swayed ever so
slightly, hiccupped, and vomited on my shoulder. "Oh, God, sorry,
Hanna. Jesus, I'm really drunk," he giggled. Sour, lumpy, beer-
smelling vomit began to run down my left breast, over the taffeta
bodice and onto the crisp black netting. I felt a warm pool
collecting in my cleavage.

Grateful that my grandparents were sound sleepers, I switched on
the bathroom light and checked the mirror for an aura. Finding
none, I stripped off my dress and showered away the disgusting
contents of Jim Grafton's stomach. Before I slept, I didn't think

about Jim, that pig in a tuxedo, or the sorry events of the past few hours. Rather, I thought about Grandma and the price she'd paid for that dress in so many ways. I remembered seeing her bent over the old portable sewing machine, yards of black material spread out in front of her on the folding card table, flexing fingers that were stiff and arthritic, taking off her glasses to rub her strained eyes. I hadn't understood how much I was asking of her.

Some people say that twins can sense each other's whereabouts every hour of the day and night. If one twin is in danger, the other one knows it somehow and springs into action, even out of a sound sleep. That isn't necessarily true. Sometimes when one twin is in danger, the other twin continues sleeping, if fitfully. When I heard Roseanna tiptoe across the floor and slip into her bed, it was nearly daylight.

O   O   O

In August, Roseanna made the astounding announcement that she and Joe Parker were getting married, and soon! Joe had been our high school heartthrob. Everyone had been crazy about him. I'd never dreamed of getting any closer to him than passing in the halls. Joe had graduated a year ahead of us. We never expected to see him at our senior prom. In retrospect, how like him to be hanging around and hoping to get lucky, and with shy Roseanna, of all people, the girl who said, "To me boys are like wild flowers. They're pretty to look at, but up close I'm allergic." People sure can surprise you, can't they? Roseanna had had her own agenda and I had been blind-sided. I never saw it coming.

You might think that a family under duress would rally together, support one another, discuss the issues rationally, reasonably. My family did none of those things. Rather, the wedding plans took on a life of their own, and my family and I became mindless as lemmings migrating toward the sea. If anyone present knew any reason why this man and woman should not be united in matrimony, we were keeping it to ourselves. Grandpa, not a man to be shushed under normal circumstances, made only this simple pronouncement on Roseanna's impending nuptials: "If you lie down with dogs, you get up with fleas." An insightful old cuss, our grandpa. As for me, I was dumbstruck and that was just as well. No one wanted my opinion. Anything I said was going to sound like sour grapes. But had anyone bothered to ask what I thought, I'd have told them Roseanna was no match for Joe Parker.

Roseanna and Joe were married by a justice of the peace on September 16, 1955. There was a small champagne brunch at the Sovereign Hotel after the service. Only family members were present, some more present than others. I couldn't seem to catch my breath. My arms and legs felt heavy. It was as if I were far away from the party, looking on from the vantage point of my own coffin.

Jolynn Elizabeth Parker was born on February 25, 1956, precisely nine months after the prom. But who's counting?

Some things in life are just too painful to face. I made a conscious effort, during the day, not to think about my sister. At night, my subconscious mind took over in dreams, searching endlessly for Roseanna in all the places we used to go together: Touhy Beach out to the end of Farwell Pier, the playground across from Gale School, and Villa Ghirgenti, our favorite pizza place up on Howard and Paulina. Every night, the lonely, fruitless search continued. It was a relief to get up in the morning.

O   O   O

Joe Parker was a piece of work. In high school, he'd had everything that mattered: devilish good looks, great body, gorgeous smile. The only child of an eccentric, adoring, over-indulgent mother and a meek, mostly absent father, Joe was self-centered beyond belief. The jewel in her crown, his mother called him. Oh, he was a jewel, all right. It would be years before Roseanna told us the gory details, but Mama and I had begun to suspect trouble right from the beginning of that unholy union.

By the time he got his hands on Roseanna, Joe's best days were behind him. He liked to say he wasn't housebroken. Roseanna soon learned he wasn't kidding. Within a few months, she discovered that Joe had two mistresses to whom he was far more faithful than he ever was to her. One was alcohol, the other, gambling. The first time

Joe stayed out all night with his unsavory friends, Jolynn was still an infant. Joe wasn't inclined to help around the house or take responsibility for the baby who cramped his style. One day, Roseanna came home from her job to find Jolynn in the bathtub all by herself. The water was stone cold, Jolynn's teeth were chattering, her lips blue. Joe was across the hall in the next apartment having a few beers with the neighbor. He had completely forgotten about eighteen-month-old Jolynn.

Joe didn't entertain any questions about his activities or the mounting bills. He took to slapping Roseanna around whenever the pressure got too high. Roseanna persuaded Joe to go for counseling. To her amazement, Joe liked the therapist. He quit drinking. He was completely sober for two weeks. By Roseanna's account, he was even more miserable to live with than before. During that brief period of sobriety, their second child was conceived, and Roseanna laughed and cried by turns, because it was so damn funny and tragic at the same time. Another baby was the last thing they needed. They could barely manage with the one they had.

When Joe fell off the wagon, he fell hard, and Roseanna was there to pay the price for every one of his shortcomings, every failure. Roseanna devised a technique to cope with Joe's brutality. She created a series of vignettes featuring Joe in the starring role, and played them in her head like a movie, to calm herself. The unifying theme was the humiliation, death, and possible dismemberment of Joe Parker.

In the first vignette Joe lipped off to the leader of a rough motorcycle gang. He was tattooed and sparsely toothed, a menacing behemoth of a man in a black, sleeveless leather vest, who proceeded to beat the living shit out of Joe. Then he unceremoniously slit Joe's throat from one side of his once-handsome face to the other. Joe fixed his terrified gaze on Roseanna, and as he drew his last gurgling breath, he wet his pants. The motorcycle guys found that part very amusing. They left Roseanna standing over Joe's lifeless body, dazed and shaken. "Sorry, lady, nothing personal," the leader said politely, and they got on their hogs and roared away.

The next time, Roseanna played that segment and added another. The vision of Joe soiling himself just at the moment of his death was so intensely pleasurable to Roseanna that she only permitted herself to use it every other segment, or every third one, for fear of becoming immune. In the stories, Roseanna was never the gun-toter, the knife-wielder, the poison-dispenser. She was powerless, a victim herself, forced to watch helplessly as the destruction took place. It was a familiar role.

The stillness of early morning was shattered when two uniformed police officers came to give Roseanna the news that Joe Parker had been shot to death outside a tavern during an altercation.

After what seemed a respectable period of mourning, it was time to get back to their normal routine. Roseanna thought Jolynn would be better off in school. The clock radio turned itself on first thing Monday morning. Roseanna woke feeling uneasy, a twinge in her abdomen. She heard Dean Martin crooning *That's Amoré*, as she discovered she was lying in a sticky, widening circle of her own blood.

○   ○   ○

The following summer, Mama came in from California. We were going to the cottage for a few weeks and Roseanna decided to join us. We invited Grandma, too, but she was having none of it. "Listen," she told us, "I worked my fingers down to little stubs in that damned cottage while everyone else was out having a good time. Wild horses couldn't drag me back to that God-forsaken place." Who knew?

Six-year-old Jolynn had grown tall and thin, and so serious. Mama and I wondered how much those big brown eyes of hers had seen. But it was lovely that year, a summer like the ones we had loved so well in our youth. Comfort Lake will work its magic on them, I told myself.

When Mama and I left that morning for the U-Pick Raspberry Farm, Rosie was on the dock thumbing through a stack of old magazines. Jolynn floated nearby on the calm, shallow water. By 11:30 it was hot on the beach. Jolynn went to get a popsicle out of the freezer. She skipped back down the cottage steps and darted past the overgrown bushes into the street. The boy saw her and stood on the brake but there was no stopping in time. He hit her solidly, knocking her flat. She looked peaceful on the pavement, they told us. The only perceptible movement at the scene was a thin ribbon of blood escaping from the corner of her mouth, and a red, white, and blue bomb-pop melting on the blacktop beside her. The innocuous-looking driver of the murder weapon huddled with Roseanna and the neighbors around the small, still figure, and wept.

Village police transported Jolynn to the hospital in Frankfort, ten miles away. We heard the sirens, Mama and I, as we ambled up and down the rows of raspberry bushes, filling our baskets beneath a brilliant blue sky. A short while later, across town, Jolynn was pronounced dead at Frankfort General.

Roseanna's conscious mind spun away to a far place, leaving someone brittle and bloodless as old bones. Mama hired Mattie Johnson to care for Roseanna until she got "back on her feet again." Mattie's job was to cook and keep house, watch Roseanna like a hawk, and give Mama a full report every evening by telephone. Mattie called my sister "Miss Rose."

For the first few weeks, Mattie reported, Roseanna remained in bed nearly around the clock, shades drawn, covers pulled over her ears, refusing food. Later, she began to pace nervously about the small apartment. She attempted to communicate by dashing off notes on a pad of paper which she flapped in Mattie's face, furious when Mattie couldn't make sense of her scribbling.

One day Roseanna drew a picture of a cigarette, ash on the end, clouds of smoke above it. On her next trip to the grocery store, Mattie bought a pack of cigarettes. Roseanna, who had always abhorred smoking, took it up with a vengeance, chain-smoking under Mattie's dubious eye. As she smoked, she pored intently over a book or magazine which she held, often as not, upside down.

Roseanna refused to go to bed at night, preferring to fall asleep fully clothed in a chair, sometimes in her coat, buttoned unevenly, purse on her lap as if ready to make a break for it. Truth be told, Roseanna was terrified of the outdoors; she wasn't going anywhere. Mattie's cheerful response was always the same when she found

Roseanna the next day. "Mornin, Miss Rose. How you doin today?" Roseanna would purse her lips and glare at Mattie.

We found a name that fit some of Roseanna's symptoms, if that was, in any way, useful. Agoraphobia is the fear of open space. More correctly, it is the fear of just about everything beyond one's own front door, beyond one's control. Small wonder, given what Roseanna had been through.

There was no contact with the outside world. She wouldn't see Mama and she wouldn't see me. Mattie was her only link to reality. Evidently, that was as much reality as she could handle. Roseanna matriculated with her demons through her own private hell. A month passed, then six months—a year, then two. Life more or less went on.

○ ○ ○

Now Mama had a notion to spend a few weeks at the cottage every summer. Warren didn't like to leave the business in California for any length of time, but he was more than willing to manage on his own for a couple of weeks while Mama visited. I was thrilled to have the company. It was a week before she told me about the x-rays. Some spots had been discovered on her lung during a routine physical. Before she left California, Mama was told she had lung cancer. As frightened as I was, I kept my thoughts to myself. Mama was doing exactly what she wanted to do, and I was just along for the ride. I felt very protective of her, like a mother must feel for her child. I took it on faith that she had once felt that way about me.

It was still chilly when we arrived at the cottage. We kept ourselves amused playing cards and board games, reading and baking chocolate chip cookies, all the rainy day activities we'd always done at the lake. We kept a toasty fire going in the stone fireplace most of the time to keep the chill away. There was no one at the lake yet. It was a quiet, serene time. Mama seemed at peace. Everything reminded me of Roseanna.

At last, we got a bit of good news from Mattie. Roseanna had finally permitted herself to cry for the first time in two years, and she'd cried as though she would never stop. A day later, Roseanna spoke. Mattie had always talked to Roseanna as she went about her daily work. "Like a cookie, Miss Rose?" she'd ask. "Want the TV on, Miss Rose?" Mattie never expected an answer when she asked, "Lovely day, ain't it, Miss Rose?" Roseanna answered "Yes." Just like that. "Yes," she said. Irresistible as the bunting of madness may have seemed, Roseanna took her first small step back from the precipice. "Yes," Roseanna said. Affirmative.

It was beastly hot in the loft. I took my pillow and top sheet down to the screened-in porch. If there was a breeze to be had, it would come there first. Before daylight, I was startled awake. Mists were rising off the lake in the half-light. It was perfectly still. I closed my eyes again, but the eerie sensation of being watched disturbed me. Suddenly, I bolted upright, staring for all I was worth through the screen door. There appeared to be some sort of shadow in the doorway, but I couldn't be sure. Overactive imagination, I told myself firmly, settling back into my cozy nest on the couch.

"So, are you going to let me in or what?" Roseanna asked, quietly.

If Comfort Lake brought up unpleasant memories for Roseanna, she never let on. Gradually, we fell into the comfortable rhythms of cottage life that we knew inside ourselves, down in our bones. We learned how to talk to each other in new ways. And if I had become a little wary by that time, and distrustful of happiness, I tried not to let it show. For all I knew, Roseanna felt the same way. She had plenty of reason to. But this wasn't about us; it was about Mama. Making her happy was all Rosie and I wanted. And she was happy— so happy that it was easy enough to forget, for a while, that she was sick.

If she was never too specific about her prognosis, I can only be grateful. Had we known, Roseanna and I would have been terrified. But Mama had made the decision to live her life the way she wanted, for as long as it lasted, without treatment. Her doctor thought she might only have six months or a year. In reality, from the time of her diagnosis, Mama had three good years and one very bad one. Rosie and I learned something utterly amazing about our mother. She was not afraid to die, not in the least. And in spite of what might be looming on the horizon, those three summers together, though bittersweet, were the happiest of times.

Things went wrong from the beginning of that fourth summer at the lake. Mama looked noticeably unwell. Her vision blurred and she began having blinding headaches and feeling sick to her stomach. Warren came immediately. We had been given a three-year reprieve. Now the horrid, insidious disease began its spiteful work in earnest, and we had to face the fact that she was going to die. There was nothing we could do.

A long illness—that's the way it's described in the newspaper. It's a sanitized way to talk about death, about cancer. It's so clean. No mention of tubes, needles and morphine. Nothing of thin, bruised skin and stainless steel pans. No talk of suffering every imaginable indignity, loss of every bodily function, every faculty.

O   O   O

I always pictured myself married some day. I thought it was what I wanted. At my age, I'm told there is a greater statistical probability that I will be abducted by space aliens than find a husband. But I don't really want a husband. I already have an intense, engaging, complicated, sometimes infuriating relationship with Roseanna. What do I need with a husband? Anyway, the marriages I've seen have been frightening propositions, at best. How can a woman be sure she won't wind up with a Ben Smith who'll roll right over her like a bulldozer, or a Joe Parker who'll try to crush her body and her spirit with his fists, or a Jack Brandt who'll take his leave of her when times get hard? The people who love us can only give what is in them to give, and it isn't always the thing that makes us happy.

Now I'm sorry for every mean, rotten thing I ever said or did to Roseanna when we were kids, though I enjoyed it well enough at the time. Now I see how much I need her. Roseanna and I have been lucky at times in our lives, and we've been unlucky, too, but always luckier together. This feels like a lucky time to me. No matter what the future holds for either of us, I'm thankful beyond words to have Roseanna back in my life, and for the tie that binds our hearts and souls in love. And for all time to come, may it be so.

(excerpt from a longer work, with the same title, still in progress)

Dale Prentiss

The Open Broken Tapping Parts

I was probably startled when my youngest brother Dean phoned on a sunny August Monday morning to say that our brother Keith, an ironworker, had had an accident. Nothing bad happened to us, not to the nine kids in our family. A couple of divorces, that's all. And nothing bad happened to big strong Keith. Some of his co-workers had fallen on the job and broken bones, and recently Keith had cut his hand on some sheet metal, but he didn't have the kind of bad luck that caused accidents at work. So I probably wasn't ready for news that Keith had an accident.

The truth is, I have no idea now what I thought about the accident news. My whole world changed with Dean's next sentence: "He's dead." "What?" "He died . . . ."

Keith, gone. People we love who die unexpectedly become even more immensely important than they were at any moment when they were alive, and their deaths can cause severe shock to those left behind. Keith's death numbed my feelings for living, and at the same time it increased all feelings of pain, all thoughts of despair, all forms of anger. All I knew was that I'd been violated, robbed of something most precious—the ability to be with someone I'd loved and known my whole life. I got hateful and lonely, even more hateful than lonely.

Sometimes good people talked to me about how our loved ones don't really leave us when they die, they just take on a new form or pass to a more peaceful place. My response for a long time was, Who cares? I don't care a bit about your theory of the afterlife, or about your theory of anything. This isn't about theories. It's about no more conversations with someone I thought I'd grow old with. It's about two families destroyed. It's about my thirty-one-year-old brother falling onto his head and bleeding and dying just a few minutes after driving his blue truck to work on a Monday morning.

The future was dark and closed off and I didn't want to hear theories. Someone I loved was buried in the dirt. I didn't want to hear anyone else's sad stories or anything about ghosts and angels.

If I wanted to hear about anything, I wanted to hear about Keith. That's all. And I could talk about grief itself, because it had overtaken my world, but only with my family and my closest friends. Any other conversation bothered me, usually more than I showed because I wasn't raised to be as miserable as I felt.

I didn't want to write either. A few times I followed someone's advice and wrote letters to Keith. That was always more helpful than just about anything else I did. But it made me feel better, and I didn't want to feel better. Out of spite or depression or anger at God, I wanted to be miserable.

Finally, though, I got tired of living without being alive. I took a writing class and started for the first time to write poems. One of the people in our class wrote a note to the rest of us telling us basically to cheer up. Stop bringing me down, he wrote. But I kept going back to topics of grief and sorrow, writing my own words of pain and darkness, and I began to crack open a few doors. Some light came through those cracks. The poems that follow are some of the poems I wrote. Some show the door cracking open. Some find me standing in darkness. And amazingly some find me standing in a bright light.

I don't know how I could have found those doors and started to open them up without poetry, without writing raw impressions and emotions down on paper. I was able to recognize myself in the words I wrote. I don't even know why writing something down solved problems that hours and days of thinking or even talking about didn't solve; I haven't returned to my former fondness for theories.

The indisputable fact is that I feel much better now than I have in the three years since Keith fell and died. And I rarely feel better than when I've just written something. That's not a theory. And it's not an accident.

I can't rewrite history, making that Monday phone call be about something mundane. But through writing sometimes I can bring Keith back, if only for a minute or two. And through writing, through the wonder of saying something on paper that turns turmoil into truth or makes music out of words, I've been able to bring myself back—if only until the next person I love dies.

From Above

I'm on the roof again.
I like it up here better. The sky
is closer, and sometimes airline pilots
open their windows and wave.
Mostly though they leave me alone.
But people on the ground always think

it's okay to talk to people on roofs,
as if that's why we're up here.
It's not.

I come here to see what I can't see
from the driveway where the concrete
broke a bottle of wine
that fell out of my grocery bag yesterday,
the driveway that lets dandelions and other weeds
grow in its cracks until I bend over and pull at them

only to hear little pops. Then I simply
lose the roots. I see the stubborn weeds
in the cracks again the next week—

unless I'm on the roof. From there the driveway
is an elegant silver-gray first surface
from my home to the world of possibilities.
Every evening I lift myself on the ladder's rungs
until I'm above the television's sound waves, away
from its ominous, hypnotic light. I find here

silence and risk, distance and magic,
the new and vital beauty of a breeze.
I fall into a soft and wise peace within.
I can fall into this place only from above.

The Courage to Know

It's always a miracle
when a water bird makes its perfect passage
from flying to floating.
I sit alone in early autumn
as drakes and ducks glide
into the cemetery's cold green river.

Suddenly, soaring with a wild animal's grace,
the great blue heron enters the ravine.
Indigo wings, spread wide as the river,
carry behind them two thin tree branches.
The heron lands and stands.

His neck is a slate-blue question mark.
Does he, on this endless morning,
wish to be among the ducks?

He opens full his willing wings,
lifts himself above the river, and flies
across the cemetery.

A Steady Stillness

The piano waits in silence,
offering up its gifts.
Relics rest on its surface:
a stained-glass angel,
four bleached adobe bowls—
two with wax, white like clouds,
two with wax, blue like heaven—
and from the funeral a dried rose,
purple like a scar.

The piano stands just where we left it
two years ago.
No one searches for a key,
so the piano waits.

Then today the waiting ends:
Jesu, Joy of Man's Desiring—
sounds from another sphere come forth
by complete surprise,
like a father's tears.

Tonight those four candles will burn,
this earthly place made radiant
by light from the heavens
and light through the clouds.
The piano will rest in splendor,
having tendered these three gifts:
a steady stillness, a sacred surface,
and a passage to the gods.

Northeast from Oak Ridge

Adrianne drives in peace, a grown-up peace
from grown-up grief.

Heavy gray clouds hover
over coffee-tan floodplains.

Linda McCartney, dead at fifty-six. So easily
we let strangers drift away.

Everywhere trees with perfect posture reach to the skies
for answers to questions I can't ask.

The redbud tree is a brilliant purple, barely caring about truth,
modesty, trucks, or yesterday.

These mountains are parents who love me,
says Adrianne with wonder. I wonder with her.

Meanwhile I trust only the oaks
stretching tall and silent on the ridge.

Postcard from Heaven

Greenly in the morning mist,
the scene outside my high window
could pass for a poster: needles

and leaves a watercolor wash,
bark a deeper darkness
interrupting. On this day

in the 1950s I was born.
I'm still fetal when I sleep,
dreaming fatal dreams of cars

crashing and empty parties.
But then I awake to the river's
rush, Cole Porter birds

sending love notes through the
homemade screen, and strong coffee
in a blue ceramic mug served up by a

cowlicked little boy whose laugh,
like the northern lights, can't be
photographed or forgotten.

At Least a Little Lost

I like to be at least a little lost,
stumbling into crumbling forests,
army-green moss clinging
to the lower branches of ponderosa pines
like fuzz on the antlers of an unruly elk.

I crash elk-like through treetops
knocked down in last October's ice storm,
all wildlife now fully aware of my adventure.
I panic a bit, knowing I could fall
and fracture some essential limb,
bone protruding through thin blood-
caked skin to point at me in ridicule.

The panic sharpens my senses:
pine needles in the sun
are brightest near the branch, and
soft as milkweed to a child's eye;
birds everywhere offer suggestions and song;
False Bottom Creek (probably) surges below
in celebration of June rains; a birthday gift
of a deer trail allows for solid footing across a ridge.

The sun shines high to remind me
that it is still morning,
that I have all today to be lost,
and that enlightenment
is another word for ceaseless discovery.

Midsummer Eve

The first time we meet
is a night of pagan festivals
and fertility rites,

a night when ghosts
and fairies become visible
and walk abroad. It is also

Discovery Day
in parts of Canada. We meet
at Ann's, where I set the table,

placing your white plate
across from mine.
My courage scares me,

but on magical nights
one tends to fight back fear
with gestures of truth. I ask

for a slice of bread,
and you oblige. I want you
to sustain me

when the rains fall
and all is clean, air electric,
grasses wet. Your subtle reduction

of many hard questions
tells me almost enough.
I fantasize the rest.

Prentiss

The dew on Midsummer Day
is said to make young girls beautiful
and old people look younger

by washing in it. I will wash in
tomorrow's dew. You, already too young
and too beautiful, can sleep late.

The Mermaid Reason

She attracts every ounce of fluid in the room.
Strands of damp hair stick to her neck
and it's a dry county. I'm in love with her neck.
My sweating water glass pulls me her way, even though
I was leaving a few swollen moments ago; even though
my weightless mind says I don't know.

She might be the only mermaid I'll ever meet.
Like a jellyfish I pulse across the room, but I'm
tossed off course by a wave of gravy-loving men,
men who wouldn't know a mermaid from a muskrat.
I see her with her seaweed soup
and show up with a ladle.

Yes, she gleams, her mouth moist.
She swims in my stream of consciousness, asking
questions that pour into answers. Soon
she slips into a coat as sleek as
sealskin and we're in a boat
gliding in silence to an undiscovered island.

Sliding out of the coat she's into the water,
where she will lead and I will follow,
holding back and then I swallow, falling,
folding, into sea.
Awash in the warm gift of wonder,
I let it go. I let it go.

Life at the Speed of Poetry

By the time Dean swings out over the water,
grasping the rope with hands, thighs, and feet,
he's already smiling inside. He doesn't care
that his release won't be perfect, or
that the springtime lake will steal his breath.

He's first off the rope swing.
He's surrounded by family.
He's already smiling.
Lunch was tomato soup
and grilled cheese sandwiches.
Adrianne dreams next to the bridge.

There's nothing to plan,
nothing to fix,
nothing else to be.
Dean finds a red kayak under the barn
beyond the threads of spiders webs.
Easing the boat into a stagnant pond
because it might be fun,
sitting cautiously now at pond level,
he loops two white paddles into green muck.
The kayak slides silently forward,

slowly into clearer water. Plop—
a turtle. And another. Dean envies turtles.
Watching an ancient snapper
he dreams up an invention,
a way to pull his neck inside his shirt
whenever necessary. Dean floats
at pond level for a month or two, slipping
white paddles into green water, dipping
grilled cheese sandwiches into tomato soup.
He pulls into and pushes out of his shell,
plops into ponds, and smiles inside.

Truce

She sees me not; but dogs recall
when I come home, barking bright
in darkling light: an unrequited
unhello. And down the hall

what she will see tonight is me
so long away. She'll whisper, *Why?*
For what good reason? None have I
but then there's me, and she can see

through every treason. Conversations
like explosions die so sweetly.
Hearts can never burst completely:
my hands offer reparations

undertaken. She betrays
her inclinations. We obey our hearts,
the open broken tapping parts
that aren't quite shattered. We say

it doesn't matter and we waltz inside
the bedspread and I wash her hair
and neck and then, when loose, she dares
to bare my wounded side.

Trip to San Francisco

We drove the lazy land last year,
dislocated. Trucks were stuck
in rearview mirrors. Blackish muck

of childish fears appeared
in spring—Indiana
oozing over all we knew.

Gray and brown Americana
washed across our happy past,
filled the car with accusation

nightmare days of indignation
everything was lost at last:
four long years of trying love,

plots inside the gnarled themes,
kindness from above. Between the blue
of two great oceans

you and me and dying love.

One Week Only

I remember moments so tender
I can't write them on paper.
I remember everything, actually,
about the last week

of a century's last summer.
And then the week ended.
It went away like Marion
in the morning. Like a radio show

on a blank tape, it couldn't be
recovered. The quadratic equation
packed its bag and flew away,
huddling in a blue stucco upper room,

wondering if a hurricane wind
would blow the island closer to land,
wondering what had happened to us.
Our one and only week, and I walked away

on shaky legs into secular days,
astonished and awkward, courageous,
contagious, and kinder somehow.
I believe I can see myself

most alive in the eyes of a lover.
I believe in love and I believe
in myself, even though this time
I got to see both for one week only.

Good Consumers

Every ghost is knocking; we are still, drawn
down below the mist until the clanging stops.
Each day is a dismal shower: buy this, buy that.
Warm and stark, in shock, we are all lost angels.

We endure the drenching; we are volunteers
racing in the shower's path,
yelling at bone-minded gazelles
and horseflies, always in dampness.

In the valley I see a traffic jam.
Saints take siege, soaked in their vehicles.
Debutantes drown in roses,
zizia showers damage the sky,
dogs and news-anchors are shipwrecked,
guests wear headsets in the diner,
and the traffic below is getting
angry and rude. In the autumntide,
under excessive Western skies,
we are either ghosts or insects.

Recent Now: Alone among Each Other

changed at four the world this afternoon
words are now so difficult from then
changed the tunes we knew to newer tunes
I can make a history of who remembers when

yesterday together we crooked walked the path
walking all the sunsets through the night
yesterday together we knew among the myth
walking all the way, lightness into light

walking all the way we stubborn learned to hear
yesterday we thought we were alone
walking all the sunsets with friends from far afar
yesterday we lived among the people in our homes

This Place Must Be Home

Sun, white and low, glows amber
on the flat waxed paper
of Lake Erie ice below me.

I peer through a 747's
wind-etched porthole. After a week away,
even the old snow below is

welcome. I drift from the plane and enter
my house. I tell my cat he's beautiful
and that I love him. At home now

I lift Vinnie to my left shoulder
where he purrs
until the plane bounces us all helplessly

onto the runway. Gravity
forces thoughts back into bodies,
but only because this mad deceleration

leaves them no choice. The voice
of a flight attendant: *We wish you*
a pleasant stay, if this

is your final destination. Even if it isn't,
I begin to look forward.

A Kid in a K-Mart Store

Mom's best escape was shopping, usually at K-Mart. A lot of mothers called it "K-Mart's," as if it were owned by someone named Kay Mart. But I was pedantic even at nine and noticed proudly that Mom took the trouble to pronounce it as it appeared on the 15-foot-tall red block-letter sign affixed to the brick wall just above the glass rotating-door entrance.

We loved that K-Mart store. And we loved individual attention, so precious in a large family. It started out to be a happy evening for me when Mom invited me along.

Inside the entrance we made a plan to meet near the cash registers in an hour. My younger sister Jodie's birthday was the next day, so I was going to get her a present. I could stretch my $4 to buy something for Jodie and something for me, I thought, as I shopped the bins nearest the door. I set out to wander the store, listening for which of the thousands of products spoke out to me in a language Jodie would understand. That's the way Mom shopped too. I never saw her with a list. The shopping helped her relax; meandering put her in neutral.

It wasn't long before I found an assortment of Wrigley's gum with white wrappers, the kind Jodie liked, for 89 cents. I picked out one for Jodie and a single pack for me. I then looked mostly at baseball gloves but also found a shirt to try on. While in the dressing room, I had an arresting thought: why not put the single pack of gum in my pants pocket?

A few years earlier, as a kindergartner waiting at the school-bus stop alone, I had ducked behind a tree before the bus arrived in order to find out just how long the driver would sit in the bus before coming to find me. She waited longer than I thought she would, and then to my amazement she just drove away. I walked back up the driveway and explained the whole thing to my mom, who told me I'd have to sit on the sofa until I learned to tie my shoes. It turned out to be a nice day—I learned to tie my shoes, and also to keep asking myself interesting questions.

I tucked away the pack of gum and left the dressing room. I shopped a bit more then headed for the cash register, thinking it was

Prentiss

about time to meet Mom. I'm not sure if I remembered the pack of gum in my pocket.

At least that's what I would tell the detective. After I bought Jodie's gum and went through the line, the man behind me took my arm.

"Don't be alarmed," he said. "I'm a store detective. I wonder if you would follow me to my office in the back of the store?"

I was alarmed. I knew I was going to cry and get in big trouble. There was no doubt, as this serious man led me to the back of the store, that I'd done something very dumb, something very bad.

When we got to a dingy brown room with cheap plasterboard walls, the man asked me if I knew what this was all about. I asked if it was about the gum. He asked if I had planned to pay for it. Then he asked who was with me. "Are you going to tell my mom?" I asked. My strategy was to stall for time until I could figure out how to erase what had happened. He paged my mom.

"I forgot about that pack of gum in my pocket, sir," I told the detective, who looked old and tired, like a typical adult male K-Mart shopper. I showed him that I had the money to buy the gum, and showed him the gum I did buy as a birthday present for my sister. How could I be a thief?

"Why don't we wait until your mother arrives," he suggested, "before we talk any more about this?"

When she walked in—my own mom walking into a room and seeing me, a detective, and an item I'd stolen—I finally cried. I was so humiliated I cried some more. Then I settled down and the detective explained to Mom what had happened.

"I observed your son going into the dressing room with two packages," he said, "and coming out with one." The detective, sitting in that room with the thief, the thief's mother, and the truth, made an offer. "Mrs. Prentiss, how does this sound? Your son can go home now if he'll admit that he'd planned to take the gum without paying for it." Mom said that sounded fair to her. By that point I'd lost the will to lie, so I admitted it, cried some more, and headed out to the car with Mom.

Down the drain went nine years of being good, and all the love and freedom that had earned me—that's what I thought about first.

152

Then I realized that the biggest humiliation was ahead of me: facing the family. We got in the car.

Mom was surprisingly calm. "I think you learned an important lesson tonight," she said.

"Yep," I said, looking down at my lap, never wanting to look up.

"Would it be okay," she asked, "if we didn't tell anyone else about your part of the shopping trip?"

I was speechless.

"You bought Jodie a nice birthday gift," she added. "I'll help you wrap it when we get home."

Rhonda Hacker

Earthquakes and Aftershocks

It's 1993. I'm about to move back to Michigan to help take care of my dad. My friend Barb tells me, "Be sure and keep a journal."

I haven't had a TV in Seattle. I've never even seen "thirtysomething" before. I have nothing in common with Hope and Michael or Nancy and Elliot, except that I'm also in my thirties. But I get hooked on the show. By the time we finish Dad's night-time routine, there's only a small window of time to jot down what's happened that day, till the nightly "thirtysomething" rerun comes on.

But gradually the network pushes the show into later and later time slots. I have more time to kill before it comes on. The words start flowing, then hemorrhaging: grief over my Seattle life, guilt for grieving it, anger at my dad's stubbornness, bewilderment when he stops nagging me to drain a dish rack or wipe the bathtub tile. And then my dad dies. The force I've pushed against with all my might for all my life is gone. I fall on my face.

I flounder in grief, guilt, love, fury, resentment, pain. I take it out on my mom. I hear my voice sound impatient, exasperated, like my dad's. I finally stumble into a writing class, open up a crack at a time. I feel foolish, but kind encouraging people say "Keep telling your stories." And so I struggle on. I still can't write about the people I love without pain of loss intruding. I can still cry when I tip the dish rack or wipe down shower walls. But I'm finally over "thirtysomething." Writing is much better therapy.

Traces of Dad

On Sunday mornings he spreads newspapers over the bedspread and lines the shoes up for polishing. The black high-tops at one end, and the browns at the other. Worn-out underwear make excellent polishing rags. He dips a rag-covered index finger into the can of Kiwi, rubs each pair from toe to heel. They lie in a line on the newspapers on top of the bedspread, like a litter of newborn puppies. He scratches their ears and strokes their backs. They sleep. Their dull black and brown coats dry through the afternoon. In the evening, the puppies awaken to a rub down. With a clean rag, he buffs their coats. They are shiny newborns again.

Most of the shirts and suits are gone now. We have given them to friends and relatives and Goodwill. But the shoes are still here, all twelve pairs of them: his go-to-Farmer-Jack shoes, his sweep-out-the-garage shoes, his work shoes, dress shoes, polish-shoes shoes. They are difficult to give away because no one else in the world can wear them. One high-top is taller than the other. It is built up on the inside and wider on the outside. His shoes hold his feet and ankles at the proper angle. They let him walk. They are made from plaster castings of his feet. Not many shoemakers around anymore can make shoes like these. There's a three to four-month wait to order a new pair. His feet are small but thick and round, like pink mangoes. The toes curl neatly, as if a sculptor tried and tried to get the toes just right and, in a fit of frustration, squashed the feet between his palms, smooshing the toes and thickening the insteps.

I still have the piece of paper I traced his feet on. They are swollen by this time and wrestling his feet into his shoes is an exhausting ordeal. The shoes feel heavier every day. I try putting my broken-in black high-top Reeboks on his feet. They go on with ease. We are thrilled.

"Me wearing your shoes," he says. "I hope this doesn't start my heart bleeding." It is an old joke. When he got my blood in a few of his transfusions, he worried it might turn him into a liberal.

I take the piece of paper to the shoe store to buy him a brand new pair of black high top Reeboks. The outline of his feet fit the soles of the shoes. But when we try them on at home, they won't go on past the insteps.

At 2:00 a.m. the last time his catheter clogs, we argue over whether to go to Emergency.

"Let me try one more time," I say. "Remember I got it flushed out last time and we didn't have to spend eight hours in Emergency." But he is adamant. We spend the night in Emergency. He wears my black high-tops.

He is stubborn, and I am furious that he is so stubborn, though I am just like him. I can't stop the calcium, leaching from his bones, that clogs his catheter. I can't unclog the catheter, and I can't stop the cancer. I can give him my shoes. I watch his Reebok-ed feet, poking out of the sheet at the bottom of the emergency room bed. They are two scared pound puppies, wondering if they'll get to go home.

Detente

"Look at the buds, Rhon!" Dad says. We drive down Eleven Mile, past bare Royal Oak oaks, to Mr. Eastham's. It's still weeks before anything turns green. Sullen preteen, I slouch in the passenger seat. Dad loves the change of seasons. I do too, but not cooped up in the car on a Saturday.

Dad steers with his left hand, gestures with his right. He finishes making his point before he pulls on the hand control to accelerate. If it's a particularly heated discussion, we slow down to barely moving, then lurch ahead as he gives the hand control an emphatic yank.

We pass woods being bulldozed for a strip mall. I am outraged.

"Development is good for the economy Rhon," he says. "It creates jobs. Trees are replaceable. You see things too simplistically," he says.

"Trees convert carbon dioxide to oxygen. Trees let us live," I say. Dad is exasperated.

"You don't understand. You don't see the big picture," he says.

"*You* don't see the big picture. The global picture is if we run out of oxygen, we die."

We argue on, voices escalating, car lurching.

We arrive at Mr. Eastham's, both furious. I try to concentrate on Chopin, but it feels pointless in the light of impending global destruction. Mr. Eastham sips his pipe. If he is disheartened by my half-hearted performance he doesn't let on. I stumble through the rest of my piano lesson.

Dad takes Twelve Mile on the way home, past Shrine of the Little Flower, and The Doll Hospital. We are silent, still seething from the strip mall argument. Dad fiddles with the radio, looking for Gershwin or show tunes. He finds a Polish station. Neither of us knows a word of Polish. He just likes the sound of other languages. I roll my eyes.

"Dad! The Dairy Queen's open!" Dad breaks hard, makes a quick left into the parking lot. I bound out of the car, grip the driver's side window ledge and jump up and down while Dad wrestles his wallet out of his back pocket. I order him a hot fudge sundae, and me a chocolate cone dipped in chocolate.

We both grin, savoring the first DQ of the season. Dad pulls out onto Twelve Mile. Polish drifts softly out of the open windows. We forget our feud. We have achieved peace through soft serve.

Travels with Mom

The saleswoman asks, *How old is she?*
I am confused. *Who?* I say.
How old is your mother?
You can ask her, I say.
She asks my mother how old she is.
My mother answers playfully.
How old do you think I am?
My mother and the saleswoman begin to chat.
The saleswoman realizes that my mother can hear and speak.
We make our purchases, maneuver the wheelchair
down the narrow isle and out the door.

The bumper sticker on his SUV reads,
I am the proud father of a Cub Scout.
He zips into the handicapped spot,
hangs a handicapped placard on his rearview mirror,
jogs the few steps to the door,
and comes out with a Sprite. I am livid.
Maybe he has a heart condition, my mother offers.
It's not a good idea to confront him. Maybe he has a gun, she says.
Listen, butthead! I yell.
Is this the example you set for your Cub Scout?
The windows are rolled up. He doesn't hear me.
My mother is relieved.

Juno

Juno whimpers at the door only a few minutes when Cathy leaves for the hospital. After a while he comes into the family room to check out the action. He is a well-behaved houseguest. He cleans the kitchen floor like a Hoover. He scours the carpet, sucking up stray bran flakes. Juno is polite and sociable. He lies at my mom's feet most of the day. Occasionally he lifts his ears to study far-off engine noises. Cathy says he knows the sound of her car from blocks away. Other cars drive down their street at home in Boston all day long, even other Toyota Corollas. Only when Cathy's car rounds the corner does Juno run to the door and wait to greet her, tail-stub wagging wildly.

We go back to seventh grade, Cath and I. She comes back to visit every year. She brings Juno. He's her baby. They stay with her mother. This year her mother's house is too empty and lonely. This year's visit wasn't planned.

We are new at doggie daycare. But Juno shows us the ropes. He looks up at us with his big yellow eyes, head cocked, one ear up at a quizzical angle. "What time will my mom be back?" he says. "How's that tuna salad you're eating? Are you sure you want to finish it? I could save you the calories."

He's a bit nervous when my mom's wheelchair moves. He chases alongside the rolling beast, nipping at the wheels. Australian Shepherds are herding dogs, Cathy explains. I doubt if Juno has ever encountered a herd of wheelchairs, but instincts run deep.

Cathy stays late at the hospital. Her mother's prognosis is not good. Juno waits patiently for supper. He tells me it's time for his evening walk. He carries his Frisbee. I hold the leash and two plastic poop bags, just in case. Juno is a champion Frisbee catcher, running fast and far, leaping into the air to intercept Cathy's graceful arcs. He is tolerant of my wobbly boomerang tosses. He fetches them without a trace of ridicule.

Home for supper. A bowl of Iams. Juno downs it in twenty-seven seconds. He lies down by Mom's feet in time to watch *Wheel of Fortune*. He's asleep before the bonus round. The pads of his paws twitch. His tail-stub trembles. Maybe he's catching Frisbees.

Juno is awake and on his paws. He's in the front room in seconds, standing on the chair by the window, nose pressed to the glass. We hear nothing. Five minutes later, Cathy is home from her painful vigil. Her face is lined with grief. Juno leaps up and smothers her with doggie kisses. He licks away her grief like so many bran flakes.

Earthquakes and Aftershocks

On the scaffold above 2nd Avenue, John tells me his stories.
He is five years old on *Kristallnacht,*° too young to wonder.
His parents are not sympathizers. But they fear
the children of the gold-cross mother next door, who would turn
them in for any hint of disloyalty. Better to go along quietly.
For safety, his parents send him to the country.

John has never seen insulation. The outhouse in the country
has no toilet paper. He tells the story
of grabbing a hunk of soft pink cotton. Later, quietly
suffering the fiberglass splinters. We chuckle together and wonder
at his eight-year-old resourcefulness.
We sit on the scaffold taking turns
holding the water-cooled concrete core-cutter,
drilling holes in old brick. We only fear

cold and boredom. We insert steel rods
for seismic reinforcement, to allay fears
of crumbling brick, in case the "big one"
hits this part of the country.
November wind and cold spray evaporate when it's my turn
to hold the drill on the second-story
scaffold of the Alexis Hotel, and John tells me
about *his* apprenticeship. It is no wonder
he is the most skilled and respected journeyman on the job site.
The factories are quiet

in bombed out post-war Germany.
At fourteen, John hikes into the quiet
forest, fells a tree, drags it back to the shop.
Ingenuity has replaced fear.
He saws, stacks, and seasons the wood,
planes it, shapes it, and creates a wooden wonder.
Our friendship outlasts the Alexis Hotel job.
We take bike rides in the country.

I help him on side jobs, hold onto his stories
and random bits of wisdom. Toothpaste will polish a teakettle.
Soap will make a stubborn screw turn.

The old world and the new never meet until the samba class. I turn
the tension rods on the drum and proudly show John
the sultry samba rhythms I've learned. A quiet
pause. He picks up the drum and plays a crisp
military rhythm. He tells me the story
of the Hitler Youth when I ask
where he learned to play the drum like that. Fear
creeps up my neck. I see flaxen-haired children
goose-stepping through the country.
He is the same man he was a minute ago, but I wonder.

Many years cement our friendship.
It comes without warning. We wonder
how this thing could happen to such a vital, energetic man. It turns
out the cancer has already spread. We still bike-ride in the country,
but his energy is waning. Mostly we sit and talk, or just sit quietly.
Over Ivars fish and chips, we talk about death, and about fear.
We cry. I tell him I will remember all of his stories.

Sixty years and thousands of miles from that country,
the anniversary of *Kristallnacht* slips by quietly.
These days I wonder, as John turns
a bowl on a lathe in my memory, how fear
turns each of us, and reshapes our stories.

°*Kristallnacht means "Night of Broken Glass." It refers to a pogrom, conducted
throughout Germany on November 9th and 10th, 1938. Jewish shop windows
were smashed, houses and stores demolished and looted, synagogues were
burned and many Jews were killed, or beaten, arrested, and dragged off to
concentration camps.*

Homage to the Journeymen

The knife travels easily if I cut the brownies before they've cooled, but globs bunch up, giving the edges an already-been-nibbled look. This batch must look its best. It's a belated birthday present for Carol. But I wait too long. They're no longer pliant obedient brownies, but hardened street-smart brownies. They resist the knife. I must cut them with a sawing motion. As I cut, ol' Swan's voice starts up in my head.

"Keep that saw steady. Concentrate on the blade," he tells me. "Make adjustments with your wrist." We are cutting compound angles of curved roof rafters on the Thai village restroom at the zoo. We sit on planks over the ceiling joists. He gives me pointers between stories about his wife who recently got fed up and left him. In the middle of Swan's advice, Bernie's voice interrupts, telling me to concentrate on the head of the nail.

"Your hand will follow your eye," he says, as I land a glancing blow that bends the nail. Such simple advice, but nobody has ever told me these things. Jens shows me how to roll up a cord without kinks.

"Hurry every chance you get," he teases in his thick Danish accent.

Dean teaches me how to blunt the point of a nail so it pierces the wood instead of splitting it. He says, "Be sure and carry an extra pair of dry clothes in case you fall in." It's February. We lean out of the boat to set forms for pier caps on concrete pilings poking out of the Sound. They are wet and slippery. I reposition my foot to get a better angle, and before I can swing the hammer, I am shoulder deep in twelve feet of ice water, tool belt and all. I thank Dean silently as they haul me out of the water.

Gene, quiet reserved Gene, swings his 22oz wafflehead, drives 16d sinkers home in two strokes. We're bent over, framing a stud wall laid out on the floor. Gene hurls his hammer and lets out an explosion of profanity. I look up to see him hopping on one leg, holding the other against his chest. He's whacked his shin. When the swearing stops, he gives me some good advice.

"Don't do that," he says.

I burst out laughing. This causes a wobble in the last row of brownies. The rest of the pan looks pretty straight. A few sides have a slight bevel, Swan would be quick to point out. But they'll pass for birthday grade. I pack them in a tin, in layers of wax paper, hurrying every chance I get.

Table Saw

The picture frame is a gift for Deb and Jay.
I want it to be narrow and graceful.
I rip the rabbet on the last piece of stock.
Fingers guide the thin strip of fir.
The blade, a silver flash,
brushes so lightly,
I'm not even sure it's happened.
Red drops spatter the throat plate.
I find the off switch, look at my finger.
The middle finger.
Not the clean eighth-inch kerf
a blade will neatly cut through a piece of wood,
but a delicate, multi-tiered array of jagged pink,
like petals of a tissue paper carnation.

It's Sunday. Nobody's around.
I search for a clean rag,
wrap my finger, close up shop,
get in the truck and drive to Public Health Hospital Emergency.
I steer with my knees when I shift with my left hand.
My right hand's up in the air
as shock thaws and throbbing begins in earnest.
In line at Emergency,
my legs begin to shake.

That was an unbelievably stupid, careless thing to do,
a voice in my head harasses me
for the next four hours
as I wait my turn.
Seven stitches, a kind doctor.

Don't be so hard on yourself. These things happen, he says.
I fight tears of embarrassment and gratitude.
All my digits are intact.

166

I drive home grasping the top of the steering wheel
with my thumb and index finger.
The gauze bandage sticks up like an albino corn dog,
flashing an obscene gesture
at each oncoming car.

Grandpa's Hands

My smooth brown summer hands wither
overnight to rough wrinkled red.
They are Dad's hands
except for the chewed nails and cuticles.
His nails are well-shaped, clipped straight.
His palms are callused where he holds his crutches,
but the backs are smooth, summer and winter.
Your hands are chapped, he tells me.
Try glycerin and rosewater.

I don't like the greasiness, I say.
My knuckles crack, fingertips split.
By mid-winter my hands are Grandpa's,
same shape, same ninety-year old wrinkles.
His hands are long-retired from woodworking,
but the curve of his cane preserves his hammer callus.
The first knuckle of his right index finger is missing,
so is the tip of my right middle finger.

Grandpa, I started my apprenticeship.
I want to be a carpenter like you, I tell him,
the year before he dies. He looks me in the eye,
pats my wrinkled hand with his.

I'd rather you gave me great-grandchildren, he says.

Tiny Tears

Grandpa measures Tiny Tears with his folding wooden ruler,
writes her measurements on a scrap of wood.
He is seventy-four. I am four.
He leans on his cane, shifts his weight from foot to foot,
shuffles from band saw, to table saw, to drill press,
to workbench in his garage-shop.
These days he would have double hip-replacements,
teach me to fox trot and lindy hop.

He cuts the curve of the rockers on the band saw,
rips two sides and a bottom to form the bed, drills out
small scalloped holes in the headboard and footboard for handles.
I play in the driveway with long paper–thin wood curls,
write numbers on scraps of wood. Grandpa has
lots of pencils. Every point is sharpened with knife strokes.
Every eraser is coated with ear wax.

We wait patiently, Tiny and I.
She is made of hard plastic.
Her skull is painted brown with textured curls to look like hair.
Her eyes gradually close if I rock her
from side to side for a long time.
Sometimes I get impatient and rock her fast, like a rolling pin,
to put her to sleep.
She's supposed to cry real tears,
but I have never seen them.

Grandpa and I don't talk much.
He doesn't tell me about his apprenticeship in *Czernowitz*,
why he fled Austria, or why he spits the name of Kaiser Wilhelm.
He doesn't tell me about the unborn son he left behind,

the wife, mother, father, aunts and uncles
who died in concentration camps,
the sisters who survived the camps,
who passed their rations through the barbed wire
to their nephew to keep him alive.
He doesn't tell me that his way to fight back is to survive,
to have children, to make sure
those children's children have children.

Grandpa bends stiffly,
puts the finished cradle down on the driveway
for Tiny to try out for size.
She fits perfectly. With one gentle push,
the cradle rocks her to sleep.
Grandpa smiles. Tiny is not his idea
of a great-granddaughter,
but I am only four.
There is still time.

Sharon

We crisscross Holland by train the summer of '75, two teenagers on our own for the first time. We buy a bag of *poffertjes* to munch on while we explore each new town. When we get tired, we find a bakery and sit over coffee and *gevulde koekjes*. "Are you sure this is ok?" I ask.

"Sure," you say. "The cookies aren't that sweet. And I know how to make adjustments."

This morning I call your mom. I ask her how to spell *poffertjes* and *gevulde koekjes*.

We live five houses apart on Sorrento. You race down the block and call through the mail slot, *"Tante Bevy, Tante Bevy,* can Ronnie come out and play?" You are three and I am five. I am older, but you are wiser. We make pajama parties. The party guests are you and me. I angle the legs of your cot so it collapses when you lay down on it. I am a bully. But you laugh and say, "Do it again."

We try our hand at tie-dying. I have a picture of us wearing identical tie-dyed yellow T-shirts. Our hair is parted down the middle. Yours is long and straight. Mine is plastered to my forehead with water in a vain attempt to straighten it.

You let me drop the tablet in the test tube for your fizz test. You show me how to match the color chart to see what your sugar is. You are newly diagnosed, but already you're a pro. You load your shot, bite the cap off with your teeth, and sink the needle like you are testing a cake for doneness.

All summer long you wear that purple bikini. Your hair is sun-streaked blond by mid-July. You know the words to the songs and the steps to the dances. You try to teach me, but I am hopelessly uncool, and no amount of plastering will keep my hair straight.

Dr. Ryan's eyes are gentle and earnest. I can see why you have a crush on him. "Neuropathy of the digestive tract is very rare," he says. Your weight plummets. Together you research every option. Your freckles stretch translucent across your cheekbones. Dr. Ryan's smile strains to match your fierce optimism. You lean on the IV pole as you walk me down to the cafeteria.

Your mother spells the words on the phone for me in her Dutch brogue.

"*Ya*," she says, "*gevulde koekjes*, Sharon loved those cookies. And the *poffertjes*, they sell them on the street corners, sprinkled with powdered sugar. I make them sometimes. I have a little mold to pour the batter in. They puff up. You remember, heh?"

I take the T-shirt out of the give-away bag for Purple Heart. It is thin from so many washings. The yellow is faded. I can barely see the tie-dye pattern anymore, but it's something to hold on to.

Drink Your Milk

I see her walking every morning as I bike to work.
She doesn't see me
because her spine is bent
like an old elm bough.
She can only see her Nike cross-trainers,
support stockings,
and a couple of sidewalk squares in front of her.
But she walks.
Exercise is good for the bones.

We've never spoken.
I wonder about her life.
Sometimes I imagine she was a famous ballerina.
Years of rigid posture made her spine rebel.
Sometimes she's a retired chef in an Italian restaurant.
Heat and steam from all the pasta
softened her spine
like a strand of spaghetti.
The truth is probably less fantastic:
parents struggling to feed the family,
milk in scarce supply,
scoliosis undetected,
or untreated.

Sometimes I imagine her spine is slowly straightening,
like the loop of an elm seedling
poking out of the ground.
We stop and talk.
She looks me in the knees.
A few months later she addresses my stomach,
then my chest.
One day she looks me in the eyes,
with perfect posture,
smiles, and hands me a glass of milk.
Drink this, Honey, she says,
and be sure and keep up that exercise.

Erma

Erma is probably in her mid to late 70's in bike years. She takes me to and from work every day. She is my trusty salt bike. Erma will never win a beauty contest. She is heavy. Her chrome fenders are pitted with rust, and her top tube is bent from the time we collided with an uncut curb, in the dark, at full speed. She sports a welded scar on her frame from that accident.

The bike path on Twelve Mile extends for two miles. A few stretches are plowed; a few are snow covered. Some businesses plow their driveways, and leave mountains of snow blocking the bike path. We curse these businesses, and swerve out into traffic to get around the snow mountains.

The bike path started out as a detour for cars when Twelve Mile was widened in 1975. That was the year Jimmy Hoffa disappeared. Rumors circulated that summer, that Jimmy's body was buried somewhere in that freshly poured concrete. But Erma and I are not thinking about that as the cars on Twelve Mile whiz past us, sometimes inches from her handlebars. Some drivers move over to give us room. Others honk, give us the finger, and try to squeeze us off their road. This is a motor suburb, after all, little sister of the Motor City, where every bicycle commuter is a threat to the economic health of the region.

A few weeks ago, Erma got her first pair of snow tires. For a bike in her 70's, that's probably the equivalent of a double hip replacement. She took to them immediately, forging through snow-covered streets like a frisky new mountain bike.

These dark mornings, as cars zoom past, spraying us with salt slush, I ride the thin strip of pavement next to the curb, dodging sunken sewer gratings and potholes. We hold our ground, Erma and I. We assert our right to share the road, over Mr. Hoffa's dead body.

Special Delivery

The dogs are the first to accept me. They don't mind that I'm short and brunette instead of tall and blond. Zeus butts his wide Black Lab head into my mail bag, digging for dog biscuits in the inside pocket. Chloe, the Golden, has better manners. She looks up at me with huge hungry fawn eyes and waits. Frosty, the Great Pyrenees, is my favorite. He puts his paws on the top rail of the white picket fence and looks down at me. "He's still a puppy," his dad says. He makes high-pitched seal sounds when he sees me coming. "It's the only time he barks like that," his dad says.

The people are slower to warm up to me. For a month and a half now, I pretend to be Sandy. "See my long blond hair?" I joke. Her customers are polite but reserved.

I am slow to learn the route, part business, part residential. Her customers are tolerant of my mistakes. But they make sure I know about them. "These people moved six years ago," they tell me. "Ya got the right address but the wrong street," or "You gave me the wrong catalog. It goes next door." I thank them, redouble my efforts to catch mistakes, and sigh in resignation. I will never be Sandy.

"Any word about Sandy?" they ask. "Wasn't she due in June? Haven't heard anything, eh?" Her customers have followed the Sandy saga, seen her through winter snow and spring rain, lugging her mail bag across an expanding stomach. "No," I say. "No word yet." We make polite conversation, mostly about the weather. "Hot enough for ya? Bet you'll be glad when this hot spell breaks. Still no word from Sandy?"

And then one morning, Dylan appears. Round, ruddy-faced baby boy. Seven pounds five ounces, the birth announcement reads. I sneak Dylan off the bulletin board, carefully wrap him in a plastic baggie, and tuck him into the inside pocket of my mail bag.

"Ahhhh! He's beautiful," the women coo. "Adorable! Chubby little guy. Such a ruddy complexion. He looks just like her, don't you think? Dylan," they read. A few pronounce it Dial-in and get snickered at by their co-workers. The men nod and smile. They are pleased but uncertain how to show it. "Pretty good little tax deduction," one says. At the salon, the proprietor passes Dylan around and offers me a piece of pastry from the tray that's reserved for clients only.

Sandy stays home with Dylan till January. I crunch through leaves, plow though snow. "Cold enough for ya?" Sandy's customers say. They give me homemade Christmas cookies, tins of roasted pecans, toffee logs, envelopes with Christmas tips. I've never received Christmas goodies or tips before. Tory, the Yorkshire, leaves me a box of truffles. Her mom signs the card.

On my last day as Sandy, I chat with customers out shoveling fourteen inches of snow off their walks. "So Sandy's coming back, eh? She sure picked a hell-of-a time. Thank you for the good service," a few say. "We'll miss you." Frosty squeals his seal bark as I round the corner. His white coat blends into the snowdrifts. He looks down at me with big brown eyes, licks a biscuit from my hand, then another, and another.

Food for Thought

My finger throbs in the cold inside a double layer of gloves. I handle the letter bundles and mail slots carefully, to avoid the snap of a rubber band or spring-loaded mail slot. I make a fist. Heat from the infection warms my other fingers.

Three-hundred metal mouths demand to be fed. Some grab a finger of my glove in their teeth when I try to shove the mail through. I curse and wrestle my hand free.

"When are you gonna learn?" Dad's voice can still shame me. He fills the sink with hot water, a tablespoon of Epsom salts, a dash of empathy, a quart of exasperation. I stand on a stool to reach the sink, put my hand in the water. He shows me how to soak it to draw out the infection. When it's gray and shriveled, he takes it in his. I shut my eyes, clench my teeth. Dad squeezes the infected finger. Blood and pus spurt out.

Sometimes a letter or postcard from yesterday's lunch gets lodged in a throat. I stick my hand down the narrow opening to clear the blockage. On warm days, when I don't wear gloves, sharp teeth scrape my knuckles.

Dad knows about infections. He tells me about pressure sores that won't heal, fester and ooze, force him to miss school for weeks at a time. And how one day, a miracle called penicillin heals the sores, lets him finish high school without getting held back a grade.

The small slots are the worst. Tight lipped, finicky, I force-feed them one bite at a time. Junk food appetizers: *Land's End, Eddie Bauer, Victoria's Secret*. Main courses too heavy to digest in one meal: *Barrons, Computer Shopper, Wall Street Journal*. High calorie desserts: *Cosmopolitan, Glamour, Vogue*.

"I saw a little girl on Maury Povich who couldn't feel pain," Mom tells me. "She bit her fingernails down so far, she chewed off a few of her fingertips. Her parents were so desperate, they had her teeth pulled to try to stop her." I wince. I've served many years of nail biter's apprenticeship,

learned the hard way how far I can chew without causing infections. I'm a journeywoman nail-biter. There's no excuse for this.

The perfect mouths have lips that part easily, wide throats that swallow lunch in one gulp. I prepare the meal as I walk up the path: *Newsweek, Harper's, Atlantic Monthly* rolled into a crepe.

Dad, I've got a government job. You always wanted me to have job security. Yeah, I still bite my fingernails. Infections? Well…once in a while. I soak 'em like you taught me: a little Epsom salt, plenty of hot water and exasperation.

I walk up an unshoveled walkway, pry open a frozen mail slot, *Family Circle* and *Life* tucked in my glove.

Thirteen Ways to Look at a Handkerchief

with thanks to Wallace Stevens

Babushka° sews clothes for the village women in the old country:
slips, underwear, wedding trousseaus, handkerchiefs.
She is the J.L. Hudson's of *Minsker Gubernia*.

Wind gusts across the deck of the ship. She ties her babushka tighter
under her chin. Somewhere in the crowd on Ellis Island,
her brother waits for her.

She dabs her eyes with her handkerchief. She doesn't love the
widower or his crippled child. But he is her brother's friend.
He needs a wife. She needs security.

She is a stern stepmother. It's boot camp and she's the drill sergeant.
Get out that handkerchief and shine those shoes, young man.

The young man stands under a canopy with his bride-to-be. A shot
glass wrapped in a handkerchief lies on the floor.
He smashes it with his crutch.

Their daughter is exuberant but messy, learning to eat with a spoon.
Mom takes a handkerchief and wipes cereal
out of her daughter's hair and nose and ears.

The oven is preheating. *Babushka* blots her forehead with her
handkerchief. Granddaughter stands on tiptoes at the counter,
hoping for a lick of batter. She watches longingly as *Babushka*
scrapes every last drop of batter into the cake pan.

Why don't you change your clothes once in a while? The daughter wears
a bandana and baggy overalls every day. Her father is exasperated.
What you need is discipline, he says. *You need to join the Navy.*

In the nursing home, he feeds soup to the drill sergeant. Gently he
dabs the drooping side of her mouth with his handkerchief. Her eyes
tell him she is grateful for his care. He realizes
she has loved him the best she can.

June heat wave. Air conditioner brownout. Dad thrashes in his
morphine sleep. The daughter soaks a handkerchief in cool water,
rings it out, and lays it on his forehead. He is slipping away.
She realizes he has loved her all along.

The young man wears a bandana like a baseball cap without a brim.
He is exuberant and charming. New things captivate him,
but quickly bore him. She is one of those things.

Why do you hang onto the past? You won't get a computer
or call-waiting. You won't even try a cold capsule.
The young man is exasperated. He reminds her of her father.
She sneezes into her handkerchief.
What? A Kleenex is too high-tech for you?

She wipes dust off the glass of old photographs.
The handkerchief is soft and familiar.

°*Babushka: 1. Grandmother 2. A woman's headscarf, folded triangularly, and*
worn tied under the chin

Linda L. Dominik

Unshuttered Windows

The table is set, the fire is laid. Petit filet mignons and miniature squash wait in the fridge. I brush my hair, freshen my lipstick, straighten the candles on the table. I expect my husband at 3:30 p.m. At 3:40 he comes in from the garage and says he has something important to tell me, but first he really has to pee. He does. Then, perched on the edge of the sofa, he says,

"You know, I've not been happy for a while and I'm leaving."

"Where are you going?" I ask.

"I'm not telling you," he says.

"What if there's an emergency? What if one of your children calls?"

"If you're in a hospital, call my secretary; she knows where I am."

He packs a bag, leaving his bathrobe and slippers, but taking the rest of the Detroit Pistons season tickets. Struck dumb, I fail to ask the question, "Why are you leaving?" I am present at the end of my life as I have known it. It is 4:00.

In the dollar-per-hour ratio, writing is cheaper than therapy, but taxes the life of illusion. As I resist every word and the emotion it evokes, writing is a push-pull Chinese finger toy—tightening as I pull away, loosening as I lean in. I am stalked by the terrifying honesty writing requires. Caught in the disclosing light, mind and body freeze. The paralysis-of-analysis produces nothing, and the goading pain does not diminish. There is only one avenue out. I reach for another piece of paper.

Maytag Moments

Laundry was done in the evenings. Elegant people took after dinner walks; we did after dinner wash.

My mother worked days in Ladies' Sportswear in McCurdy and Company, arriving home around 6:12 p.m. She got off the Hudson Avenue bus a block before or a block after our street, walked around the corner to our house. It was the first or second house on Reed Park, depending on whether you counted the corner house which faced the avenue, but whose porch faced the street.

Park was a misnomer; there was no grassy strip. It was a one-way street with only enough room for parking on one side. It had one and two story houses; all had cellars, some with outside trap doors. You could bring wet laundry out that way, if the door didn't fall on your head while you carried the basket.

This worried me a lot because the trap door was held in place with only a hook-and-eye lock. What if it pulled out of the house siding as I emerged carrying wet sheets or my dad's shorts? Who'd want to be crushed beneath laundry, even clean laundry? This was only a warm weather hazard. In winter we hung wash in the cellar.

Our cellar was a regular honeycomb divided into a fruit cellar, a coal cellar, a concrete cellar and a dirt cellar. I never went there, on the other side of the steps. Mounded like graves, the brown dirt hid things that liked darkness.

We used different parts of the cellar in different seasons. In summer we canned and filled up the fruit cellar. In winter we used the laundry cellar for drying clothes. The Maytag lived there—white with red trim, the wringer swiveling east, south, west, never north. The Maytag never moved; only the wringer moved and wrung.

"Never, ever put your hand in the wringer," said my mother with such ferocity I believed it could flatten bone, sinew and muscle in just one pass. It flattened heavy Turkish towels, bathrobes and rugs. Jeez, what was my hand in its maw?

It was electric and therefore uncontrollable. If it once got hold of my hand, the only way to stop it would be to pull the plug out of the socket above my head, which would be impossible because my hand and arm would already be sucked in and flattened. By the time the rollers reached my shoulder, I'd be too short to reach the plug! I'd be trapped, rolled-out dough.

I never put my hand in the wringer.

Dominik

Lines on Lines

Like childhood hopscotch,
my life lays itself out on
pavements, chalked spaces
broad or narrow of my making.

Lines that frame
my life hinder me
when I run or hop from
picture-framed stops.

Beginning again invites
an end. Imagination, the scissors
of my mind, says there are no ends.

I skip smooth stones to destinies
unknown. The wildest
and most fulfilling
just beyond the lines.

Ghost Mother

Dominik

You are always there, and never there.
Wind moves leaves, revealing its presence.
Your full-figured, ample, pleasingly plump
fleshed presence
                    belies absence.

The always-on radio playing
Stella Dallas and Our Gal Sunday,
buffers my voice
intruding in your reveries,
                    fantasies,
                              how-it-could-be's.

I speak, pulling you back to here . . now . . .
a backyard-tethered dog's illusion of freedom
gone, as the leash snaps taut.

Not now, Mommy's getting ready for work.
Not now, Mommy just got home from work.

When?
Never.

Your ghost tucks me into bed
as I hear the echo of your laughter
at *I Love Lucy's* foolish antics.

Children's Hospital, Palestine 1914

Mosquito-netted beds fill the room. Gauze-draped, they cocoon their patients, each a chrysalis of hope. Light and dark play along the stone floor. Dust motes, moved by the gentle Mediterranean breeze through now unshuttered windows, tell the sun's journey through the room. Its warmth comforts and coddles, like a caring mother. The glass kerosene lamp, suspended from the tall ceiling, waits its turn. It will beacon the night, as full-skirted nurses sail from bed to bed, quieting, tucking in, touching.

The children's ward, where everything but the presence of death is scaled down. It looms in its disguises—malaria, pneumonia, malnutrition—shadowing the corners remote from the sun. It overwhelms the chairs and tables, the dressers and night stands—its appetite huge.

A soft sigh, and then another, and then more. Like an orchestra assembling and tuning, the children awaken from naps, each sounding his own note of hurt.

" Ima."°

"Water"

"It hurts!"

The nurses glide, their skirts billowing, their passage marked by the chink of pitchers as they fill tumblers, touch foreheads, and rearrange tiny limbs.

The doctor enters, tall and stately in white, and death shrinks into the corner, gnaws its own emptiness a little longer.

° *Hebrew word for "Mama"*

The Bishop's Visit

I was in the eighth grade, having been confirmed a few years earlier, and Mother Superior chose me to greet the bishop and give him the roses. She said she wouldn't be there to observe the presentation, but she relied on me. I was one of the best memorizers in class, and I had nice clothes and enough poise not to trip over my feet. I memorized three short paragraphs that were hand-written on a 3x5 file card and recited them over and over to her satisfaction. She patted me on the shoulder; the burden had been laid.

The side entrance to the rectory had three steps that led to the kitchen, where the pastor's niece and housekeeper met me and took my coat. The linoleum in the rectory kitchen gleamed from hours of hands-and-knees polishing. Its waxy smell threatened the fragrance of the dozen long-stemmed red roses I cradled in my left arm.

The bishop had arrived for Confirmation, and the honor of our parish was at stake. Our priests weren't from the Diocesan seminary; they were Polish Franciscans from near Buffalo, not exactly insiders. Our parish, Saint Theresa, the Little Flower, didn't have parishioners with one syllable names, like Smith or Jones, and only one member of our church had a Cadillac, the local funeral director. High Mass at 10:30 was unintelligible to the younger members—the liturgy in Latin and the sermon in Polish—but the vestments, the incense, and the music transfixed us all in a mystery of faith.

As I stood in the rectory kitchen, I could hear convivial voices wafting in from the living room, where I was going to give my welcome speech and the roses. Suddenly the door opened, and three men walked into the kitchen—the bishop, our pastor and his assistant.

Bishop Lawrence B. Casey was well over six-feet tall. He was slender, with hair as white as the lace on his vestments. His floor-length purple cassock—lace, linen, silk—was as regal as his bearing, and the sound of rich cloth moving filled the kitchen. My eyes and mouth both opened to protest,

"What are you doing in the kitchen?" The housekeeper tugged at my sleeve, and I followed her in a genuflection, as we each kissed his Episcopal ring, honoring his office. Mother Superior hadn't planned on the silence, which lay thick as the wax on the floor.

"Are those for me?" he asked, eyeing the roses.

"Yes, Your Excellency." The flowers leapt from my hands.

"And I suppose there is a little speech that goes with them?" The interrogatory rise of his voice invited my performance. I knew it was over then. I could not think of one word.

"I'm sorry, Your Excellency. I can't remember it."

"Well, let's see. Did it start 'Dear Bishop' or 'Your Excellency.'" He tried a few more promptings. Nothing. Not a word came to me. An easy smile lit his face the whole time, his Irish eyes full of blue-sky light.

"Tell me. Which high school will you be going to in September?"

"St. Agnes, Your Excellency."

"That's great. I'll be coming out there to say the Mass of the Holy Spirit in the first week of September. When you see me, just give me a big wave, 'Hello.'"

His blue eyes rained mercy on me. I could not look into the eyes of the others. I walked to my home around the corner and found the 3x5 file card on my bedroom dresser. I did not tell my mother what had happened; I just went to bed.

○　○　○

The next day Mother Superior called me out of first period, her face crimped small by the starched wimple, her eyes wide with anticipation. She took me by the arm and walked along the hall.

"How did it go?" The chasm opened.

"I forgot the speech." It closed over me.

She said nothing, her eyes narrowing in disbelief. Her grasp on my arm tightened.

"I'm sorry. I am so sorry," I whispered. Her eyes, thin slits now, matched the line of her lips. She let go of my arm and walked away.

○　○　○

The first week in September, Bishop Lawrence B. Casey said the Mass of the Holy Spirit for the Saint Agnes High School students.

Several hundred girls in maroon uniforms sang *When Irish Eyes are Smiling* and waved happily. One Polish girl sang louder and waved harder.

Therapy Session

A well so deep,
dark so black,
not even a hope of light.
Deeper and deeper I fall.
Resigned, I must be here.
The way out
is not back up.
Up is only a breathing break
on the required journey.

You just have to sit with the pain,
says the guide.
How long is enough?
Cup of tears running over
and over
and over.
The black-holed emptiness heavy,
a Sisyphean rock.
No end.
Not today, anyway.

Sabotage

Some cut their flesh,
others beat themselves.
Starved for soul food
they deny the body meat,
their own withering to nothing.
Or stuffed like the fatted goose
fated for slaughter, futile feeding
never slakes the hunger.

The mind meanders the thought-rutted path,
falling into each pain-filled trough.
Rising more slowly each time,
the will weakening,
the bruises blacker,
the scrapes bloodier.

Self-inflicted death
comes so slowly.
The will to do it might die
before the victim.
There could be hope.

Dominik

Cemetery Journey

How shall I find the far away, lost selves of my being
scattered in the many cemeteries of loss?
Abandoned selves, casketed narrowly, await interment
in an earth of disappointment.

I am mortician and gravedigger both.
I prepare the corpse and spade the earth.
All rituals of death are in my hands.

Life wanes;
expectations diminish.
I accept less and less.
I say yes when I mean no.

Each self is not lost but sent away
to preserve an illusion.
Each self is buried hoping the bare bones that remain
will be acceptable—
I walk on the soft soil of the grave's edge,
a fragile balance.

The truth is: I damn near kill myself,
but I do not.

I visit scattered cemeteries
claiming casketed selves.

Casting Call

I don't remember being placed on stage
with a script I don't want,
a director I can't see beyond the footlights.
I don't even remember the casting call.

I stand on the bare boards,
work-light dim.
A disembodied voice lost
in the empty orchestra seats' blackness
tells me why I
won't get the part: I
don't
haven't
can't
ever do it right.
My entrances are
too early, too late,
my interpretations not the author's
and and and
and then I get it.

I don't want
      to act;
            I want
                  to be real.

The Bond

Silence
settles softly on twined limbs
like manna from a nurturing sky.
Silence
      seeps into bodies
            just fevered with passion
now cooling with the slurry of slowing breaths.

Sated,
      desires served
          subside now.
Damped fires promise flame again.

Does flesh bond souls?
Can connection forged in heat
withstand the tears of gnawing life?

Never Too Late

For all the pennies, nickels, and dimes I threw into wishing wells, my parents could have bought me a bicycle. They didn't. "Why would you need a bicycle?" my mother asked. "We take you with us everywhere we go." Where would I go without them? Not to the store for a comic or an ice cream cone. Not to the library. I continued to wish in a lot of wells, but it was my cousin, Roger, who got the bike. "Well, he's a boy," my mother said. My father said nothing.

I liked the rumble a bike made with a playing card and a clothespin on a spoke, and I really liked the multi-colored streamers that mysteriously sprouted from the handlebars. They came from inside the bars; how did they do that? I wanted a bike basket with colored ribbon woven through it—pretty like three-flavored ice cream.

"We wouldn't know where you were, if you rode away on a bicycle," said my mother. My parents had all their eggs in one basket; I was an only child. Christmases and birthdays rolled by, but I didn't roll anywhere.

At forty-two, I had a bicycle appear in my life. It had been outgrown by a lover's son. A three-speed, blue Schwinn with touched-up paint, pumped-up tires, a greased-up chain—it was mine, but I didn't know how to ride it. Phyllis offered to teach me. She was a good friend, a therapist five years older than I. She knew what this was all about.

One sunny Saturday I drove to her house. The bike was in my trunk, a bungee cord holding the trunk lid down snugly. I had no streamers, no card on the spoke, no basket—just a bell on the handlebar. Setting me up to ride, we tried to put on training wheels, but they didn't work. Phyllis just smiled and put her hand on the back of the seat, "Get on."

I rode up and down the sidewalk, while Phyllis ran along steadying me. We blushed at the sight of neighbors watching, then giggled. I couldn't seem to stop except by jumping off and slamming my feet on the pavement, the pedals slapping my calves each time.

We smiled a lot as we loaded the bike back into the trunk. We drank some wine as pink as our faces, then giggled some more. We decided that bicycle riding might be a lot like sex. Once you learn it, no matter how late in life, you never forget how.

I wore black and navy pantyhose to the office for the next three weeks. The bruises faded, and I eventually lost both big toenails, but I never forgot how to ride.

Ankle

Dominik

for Susan Chamberlin

My ankle turned more than one eye,
seductress in silk,
its curve leading
upward, the promise of more leg
lost at a hemline.

Crossed, pale ankles
mark the spot where
journeys begin.
South, feet lie poised,
take me to

        streets

            stairs

                stores

                    sanctums

where ankles
describe circles of boredom,
wind-up toys running down.
North, legs
lead to terra incognita.

Stockinged
socked
dog-collared beneath
skirted poodles,
the ankle's fashion history reveals
function: connection.

Ezekial connected the foot bone
to the ankle bone
to the leg bone
forever uniting purpose and form.

Dominik

Feet and legs

         go

                nowhere

without ankles.

My ankle,
now a blue-veined map
of journeys taken,
can still seduce with promise.

Summary Piece

"You sit here because your legs are short and will just reach the cooler." I loved the summer Saturday and Sunday escapes from the city and the ordinariness of life. The chores came to an end and the week-long expectation came to a climax as the trunk slammed shut. Dad assigned places on the basis of what else needed to go into the car. The length of legs and the width of torsos were serious factors. There was a well-developed strategy for loading the car, and my father had mastered it through much practice. The legs of the grill came off and folded up inside. The fly rod disassembled into three parts and nested on the rear window shelf. Over the years the pattern became established. It was part of the ritual, like the holy water font in the vestibule.

Our car rides seemed terribly long. Perhaps they were. Travel was two-laned then. The highway system was still only a design on some engineer's drawing board. Sometimes we'd see landmarks, like Burma Shave signs, and know how far we'd come. Our plaintive "When are we gonna get there?" calls lessened; our expectations heightened.

And then we were there! "Everybody carry at least two things and maybe we can do this in one trip!" The less desirable picnic locations weren't for us. We'd scouted out good spots years before and returned to them again and again. "No, no, it's here by this tree, with a level place for the grill. Remember, the other one was too close to the trash can." We nodded our heads in assent and strained our muscles lifting the cooler yet a few more yards.

The day unfolded like the blankets and tablecloths. Build the fire, cook the food, eat, clean up and disband to favorite activities. Off to the pier with fishing poles, onto the blankets with *Good Housekeeping* and *Ladies' Home Journal*, into nests made for naps. Furtive whispers, well out of adult earshot, "Do you wanna climb the ant hill?"

The car, warm from the sun, cocooned us as dusk made us drowsy, our eyes heavy from a day of air, water, sun, sand. It was always shorter getting home. Magic worked on a contented body whose soul was fed again and again on summer Saturdays and Sundays. The separate parts came together, all of a piece.

Maureen Dunphy

Stardust from the Barn

The first sensation of something gone awry is one of losing all control. My view of sky shifts from the waterline at the horizon to the glare of sun swimming overhead. I see my two feet flung up above me—apart, like cut-outs on a collage—just before the back of my head smacks and bounces up from the endless stretch of algae-slick limestone that is Pelee Island's South Bay. A missed beat of time passes; the rhythm of shallow waves begins nagging against my right side.

My husband pulls me from the water, and I promptly fall deeply asleep. He cajoles and half-carries me the quarter mile through woods to the car. The island clinic's nurse, flashlight in hand, notes the sluggishness of my left pupil and calls to delay the evening ferry to the mainland. At the hospital in Leamington, I drift in and out of the shaking aftermath of shock and experience nausea at every bump of my wheelchair. After x-rays reveal no skull fracture, the ER physician, diagnosing concussion and whiplash, orders two Tylenol and an injection to restore my physical equilibrium. Later we check into a cheap motel, where an alarm wakes me every two hours, so I can groggily report to my sleeping husband that I am not unconscious. After a stormy ferry ride back to the island in the morning, I finally get twelve hours of uninterrupted sleep.

Now I'm sitting in the old Mission rocker: alive, conscious, back "home," but feeling totally disconnected from who I was a mere twenty-four hours ago. I suspect the sensation is what psychologists might refer to as "disassociation." It feels more like "displacement." I am here, but not quite connected to where the *I* in relationship to *here* was before. The needle has been bumped, has jumped a number of vinyl grooves, and I am suddenly listening to another song, in which I can't quite locate the melody. I have no words to articulate how I feel, nor do I know what I need to do to return to—or even if I can return to—living the life I inhabited yesterday.

What I do this summer day—sitting in the old Mission rocker at the front window of the summer house we share with another family on Pelee—is reach for a blue Uni-ball roller pen and my writing practice notebook. My 8-1/2 by 11-inch spiral notebook with cream-colored pages and a black marbleized cover has lain fallow for a long time, waiting for me to finish an editing project, revise a piece for publication, design two new writing courses and a series of workshops, the latter of which are, ironically, on journaling.

I open the notebook. My last entry is dated "April 30," over three months ago and before I weathered the end of the school year, put in my garden, and lost my dear grandma. I remove the pen cap and write: "Concussion and whiplash," then try to describe this feeling of displacement. After twenty minutes, I take two Advil and lie down, taking the weight of my aching head off my neck. When I wake up and feel like I'm not really in my body, I pick up my notebook, read the new entry and write some more. Although I still can't quite define this feeling, I find myself, in the act of writing words, slip briefly back into myself.

Forty-eight hours after my fall, still feeling displaced when not writing, I decide to join my family at a potluck dinner with three other families at a house across the road from the lake. We sit in chairs pulled up to a long table, which is set between two trees on the front lawn. Platters of food, set atop a variety of colorful woven cloths, weigh down the table. I soak it all in and savor the images—the dappled light, nub of cloth under my fingers, aroma of Lynn's homemade spinach-cheese pie, tang of retsina on my tongue, rhythm of waves washing against the beach. I make mental notes to be added to my notebook later. How might the slivers, shadows, sounds of this dinner fit into my new novel?

Something suddenly shifts. The ways of writing pull my feet back onto the path I was traveling before my fall. The entry in my journal that begins "concussion and whiplash" brings me back into focus. What is happening now is what often happens when I put pen to paper amidst the displacement of daily life: I return to my self.

Bad-Hat Brew

During a dream journey,
the late-night bottle of beer
becomes a stone in my shoe,
your wet kiss, a bowl of cereal,
your late-night whisper, a hurricane.

My hair winds down
a pebbled path of anguish.
This tight deadline for resolution
becomes a speeding truck,
my only road map,
an abstract painting of the galaxy.

When I awake,
the buzz of the fluorescent light overhead
is a yellow jacket trapped,
is the crinkle of brown paper
wrapped around a time bomb.

"Frost Heave Ahead"

from a road sign in Vermont

You wake up early from a dream
of opening a door to a basement room
and finding a black feathery spider,
larger than a dinner plate,
crawling, leg by leg,
out of the heart of the furnace.
You scream and scream
until you can't breathe, and
as you watch, the spider turns
into a scampering black squirrel.
It is still dark between
the slats of blinds, but now
you are afraid to go back to sleep.

Before dawn, you haul one decade
of *Better Homes and Gardens*
from a ledge in the basement
out to the curb.
Once inside, panting,
your back against the slammed door—
praying for rain before you change your mind—
you suddenly recall
the fifteen years of outgrown children's clothing
still mildewing in the basement below.

On the third trip to the Salvation Army
with the last three of the fourteen garbage bags
of "usable clothing only," the
final bag splits its seams as you
shove it through the chain-link opening
to the collection cart, let it drop;
it explodes with your expelled breath.
You imagine telling anyone who asks

that there are so many bags because
the mother of the family has been sick
for a very long time.

Back home,
you breathlessly call all the men
whose numbers you have collected
on scraps of wedding reception napkins,
torn-off corners of newspapers.
Electricians, painters, wallpaper hangers,
a drywaller, a carpet installer
begin arriving with drop-cloths,
paint and paste, brushes and rollers,
ladders, and radios all tuned to oldies stations.

The painters and wallpaperers scrape and
sand the walls bare while you cough and
sift through the boxes, baskets, folders of bills,
the two grocery bags of unopened mail,
pay the overdue subscription bills
from stopped magazines,
balance three checkbooks,
file away last year's taxes,
send the children's last year's school portraits
to the out-of-town relatives, and
leave the paperboy his Christmas tip
although it is the middle of July.

You order three sets of Pantry Pest Traps
by phone from a catalog and pay double
to have them shipped express, and sighing,
throw out all the grain-moth-infested food
except for the small collection of
canned goods and unopened jars
that you leave out on the counter,
serving their contents for breakfast,

lunch, and dinner until all the cans and jars
are in the recycling bin: canned peaches,
fruit cocktail, applesauce, tomato paste,
blueberries, black olives, and baked beans.

You call the tree service and ask
to have all the dead wood removed.
They do so loudly. It is a sound that calls
for constant attention like a baby crying from
the plane seat behind you on a long flight.
You extend your exhales to match the drone.
During the tree-trimmers' lunch break,
you call an out-of-town realtor,
make an appointment to have the house appraised.

You finish digging up the front lawn,
but do not plant the garden.
The freshly turned earth dries to dust
in the yard, dries to dust on your skin.
At night, when the workmen leave
and everyone is asleep, you stand
in the shower until the hot water runs out,
then float through the dark
to sit out on the balcony staring
at the one star amidst oak leaf shapes.
You catch yourself,
between breaths,
waiting to see
what will happen next.

Spousal Surgery

My husband has been given the number 51.
The monitor reports number 51
is scheduled for surgery at nine o'clock.
It is nine o'clock.
The woman sitting next to me in jeans
and blue strappy sandals
is crying.
I am not.

I am thinking I should be holding him in my heart.
But I have forgotten the magic symbols,
cannot remember the passwords to prayer.
So instead I hold the moment of this poem tightly.
I want these words to be shoreline in morning air
punctuated by an ellipse of blue heron,
the regular rush of wave, brush of wing,
but instead I find myself on a mountaintop ledge
with a view that makes me dizzy.
I realize I am feeling the anesthesia seeping
through the tendrils by which we are still bound,
vibrating the web on which we travel together.

I desperately gulp mountain air and find myself out,
leaning against sun-warmed bricks
where the young surgeon finds me by calling out
my husband's name, which I do not share.
I look at the sheaf of photos,
the interior of my now-recovering husband's injury.
The photos are excruciatingly clear,
but provide me with no clues,

his tendons and ligaments no map,
even now, for getting down to the water
to watch the dark silhouette
of a solitary bird in flight.

What Is Still Needed

I dream we are all playing
croquet on the Fourth of July
in the rain and tall grass
with Emily Dickinson.
Apricot-walnut muffins
cool on the sill of an open window
outside Homer, Michigan.

I have stopped on my way
to the Birch's Driftwood Cabins
where I was headed in search of
Grandpa Klotzbach's white fishing cap.
I want to put it on and remember evening's
sand thud, heavy clank of horseshoes,
sweet gasoline waves churned by an outboard motor
wafting up toward wings of sunset colors
to what looked to be heaven,
the heft of firefly jars of stars
and of the feelings behind
the black and white fading smiles
we uncoiled, developed together
in the very darkest dark.

But I never got there.
When I awoke,
I was sipping a tepid cappuccino
at the Maple Valley Café,
pulling up those thick red wool socks,
jotting a list of what still was needed:
an atlas of the ancient maps,
compasses—both kinds,
sage for subtlety, rosemary
for remembrance, more thyme,
always, and my one friend
who can hear the full moon rise.

In Our Prayers

for Madaline Venette Bateman Klotzbach

The second time I changed
Grandma's diaper was easier.
See my beloved grandmother.
She turns, and all those things she never said
are melting on her tongue, but I hear
The doctors all die too, Sugarlamb.

Pausing in gentle struggle
with her slight form—
her lips are closed, not moving—
I clearly hear
Calm breath, unruly breath,
I go under to rise.

Don't fight the un-becoming,
that beckoning gaze.
This up and down rinsing,
done and undone baptism. Look,
see the wash from the Seine
hanging along the bank.

During the long broken nights,
to reach the logic of the sea
takes a fortnight of washing.
One must hasten, only to lie so long
waiting for the warmth of ice floes.

They're all forever off in their guessing,
but talk along the riverbank finally stops.
Wrapped in an animal fur,
hushaby, Gramma, rock sweetly now.
Once your blood freezes,
cutting short the jump

of salmon across weir,
with your final trochee, know
the wandering Seine will grow fuller and
for a moment, the raft-hands will gaze
with yearning toward the lamp-lit houses,
then beyond the lines as they
dabble at night mirrors of dust.

Dizzy with the wand's spin,
we may waltz in ermine nets,
but die washing to the coming end.
Only war ranks below slow decline;
don't lag back, Grandmother.
Rein in luck here, grab glory now.
While the sweet smell of urine
permeates my afternoon,
dive down deeply,
hang-glide through fine stars.

Onion Shortcake

for Meagan Mná on the occasion of her 16th birthday

Someday soon, I will tell my daughter the recipe:
Begin at home, alone.
Remove your shoes, your socks.
Preheat the oven to 425 degrees.
Measure out a full-moon glass of Merlot
made from grapes grown somewhere
you can imagine belonging.

On a breadboard at the kitchen counter,
as the sun is going down,
peel and slice ten medium-sized white onions.
But if you haven't white, or haven't
quieted yet enough to remember this detail,
yellow will do, will do no harm; make do.
Sprinkle them with 1/2 teaspoon of salt
culled from your tears.

Put on some music,
and in a saucepan over low heat, watch
the swirling of three tablespoons of butter
melting. Add the onions.
Cover and simmer until they are tender.
Dream over and check them frequently
with a wooden spoon; let the steam
escape, fill the room. Cool them
in your great-grandmother's blue china bowl
while you prepare half a recipe of biscuit dough.
Omit the sugar. Use one cup of flour,
1-1/4 teaspoon of double-acting baking powder
—the double-acting is what is hard—
take a sip of wine, you'll have the tears for
5/8 of a teaspoon more salt.
Sit down on the shadowy step
to put on your shoes. Walk
to the store for 3/4 cup of cream.

Take a sharp pair of scissors;
cut some red poppies from the border of your walk.
Put them in something cobalt blue
before adding 1/8 cup butter
made from the cream poured
into a clean mayonnaise jar
and shaken by a circle of fourth-grade girls
on a spring morning with sun slanting into the classroom.

Spread the dough; press it
with the tips of your fingers
into a greased, fired, deep dish.
Cover the dough with the cooked onions.
Now, run out in the gathering dusk,
barefoot this time,
and from the Hungarian gypsy woman,
get 1/4 teaspoon of paprika, ground
from the nightshade fruit of the capsicum;
get it in trade for a song sung *a cappella*
or the rolled canvas of an oil painting
or an unrhymed poem written that night.

Add two teaspoons of parsley grown under ice,
picked from an island garden
in a first-day-of-spring blizzard.
Firmly chop it in memory
of the island, the storm, the ice.

Add a grating, a twist of nutmeg
or white pepper depending
on the location of the grape vineyard,
the beat and harmony of the music,
the man with whom you exchanged a glance
in the dairy section. In a pinch, mace would do.

Light sixteen candles
and prepare the cream sauce:
one tablespoon of butter, two tablespoons of flour
for the roux; stir for three to five long minutes.
Very gradually add one cup of milk
stirring, stirring, stirring constantly,
your bare feet planted solid,
until you've drained your glass,
until the sauce is as thick as the story of your life.

Then add a very small onion
studded with the nails of three whole cloves.
Tear a bay leaf with your teeth,
put one-half the leaf in the cream sauce,
crumble the other half, and put it in your pocket.
When you remember,
while you're still alone,
stick your hand in your pocket,
pull it out, and smell your fingertips.
The fragrance will remind you of
things you didn't know you ever knew.
Then dip your forefinger in the pan
and taste the sauce.
Lean against the counter
and listen, listen to your tongue.

Into the sauce, beat one egg.
Pour the sauce over the onions.
Bake for years,
until the dough is done. Serve
the shortcake to your sweet daughter
on her sixteenth birthday
and tell her the recipe:
open to no man
unless he stirs up memories
of stars wheeling in deep night sky
over a place you'd almost forgotten.

Earth

In the July of my fifth decade,
I am earth:
a thrust-up wall of limestone and granite
glittering with crystals of black mica.
Air sucks through my unmortared cracks.
All rises up around me.
Lichen over my surface,
thunder in the tops of the trees,
green mountain against gray sky,
I am solid.

But here, forget-me-nots push up
from my hairline cracks,
back-lit by flashes of lightning
reflecting off the dark varnish
of my bedroom door where
my father's silhouette would appear,
would tell me that thunder was
the angels bowling in heaven,
as my grandmother had told him.

The balls rolling down
from the mountaintop,
lightning luminating the limestone
from within,
the lichens waiting,
waiting for rain,
tiny mouths open.

Particles of Shimmer, Wave of Spokes

A monsoon, perhaps?
Two kayaks adrift
on the barn's shed roof.

The soccer field
squishy
between dandelion goals.

In the middle of the path,
two freshly dug holes,
abandoned crayfish burrows.

A cardinal's cadence,
fluttering riffs snagged on
newly leafing raspberry cane.

Below, broken hulls of last year's gourds,
shovelfuls of seed, the music
of scattering rosary beads.

Suspended above, vibrating flecks,
the choreography of gnats,
particles of light and shimmer

until a flash of white,
a startled doe throws herself heedlessly
into the wave of the present.

The ripples out from the heart of things
freeze, disconnect, vanish
until a blue jay in cedars
opens the squeaky gate:
bedstraw, cleavers, wild madder.

Ring the heavy wild bell, Sweet Woodruff's cousins.
Do you know you make parasols in Paris spin?

Birdseed Offerings

New aluminum pie pan full
atop a blue plastic milk crate.
From wood-stove rocker warmth, I wish,
for wheeling flocks: juncos, starlings—
startled, now to be returning.

I hesitate to let the cat out
though the fire will be gone to ash
and I will be days off the island before
these seeds contain enough wind and sky
to attract any one lone bird back.

In an edge of ember, I dream you,
across the road from makeshift feeder,
living at the house long boarded up,
find I have written "you," stoked the fire.
At the stovepipe, a first rush of wings.

Ode to Hestia

When winter is almost over,
I take up the smooth wooden-handled broom,
warm from its wait
in a square of growing sunshine,
and I begin to sweep the year
from the corners of my house:
last summer's poppy pollen brushed in passing
glittering grains of beach sand brought home in canvas shoes
splinters of wood from the kindling of fall fires
confetti of melted candlewax
tiny amber beads of spilled perfume oil
echoes of woodpeckers in the morning fog
salts of evaporated acid rain
motes of unshared secrets
faintly glowing shards of radioactive fallout
dried crumbs of chocolates never received from lovers
curls of thyme and rosemary from never-prepared feasts with friends
whispers of disconnected late-night phone conversations
seraphs of the nouns and verbs of poems not written
filings from the keys to unopened doors
dendritic prints of unidentified fingers
flecks of dried moonblood
bits of shed skin
swirls of hair pulled from the brush of days
glimmers of almost-forgotten morning dreams
slivers of crystal from the earth's mantle
tremors of sub-surface faults
minute upon minute drift of stardust from the barn
and in the whirlwind of the straw whisks
the exquisite breaths of ghosts and angels.

Knowing

So very rarely in the deep night,
maybe only once under a blue moon
in the very deepest night:
foghorn.

Like the familiar, but forgotten
lines of a ghost story
told by a favorite grandpa,
it reverberates up from the gut,
absolute as whisker stubble,
arriving just before sleep
steals the rudder.

Finally,
through the mist,
sound pushes out an exact path;
the soul listens with braille fingers
stunned by a slice of wave-washed light.

Brushpile in a Clearing

I am the brushpile in a clearing.
Husks of last year's dried stalks
of weed wave, rattle above me,
sky-jumble of sapling trunks,
trill of insects.
Small nocturnal animals turn
in their sleep in my beds of leaves.
In the earth, beneath my belly,
creatures, deep underneath, burrow
and plow bits of root and earth.
I am the energy of a forest waiting.

I am filled with warbler flutter and song.
New grass pushes, rears through me.
Wild roses ramble, snake around me,
and wind juggles last year's tiny hips.
The rut of a small path
snared by shoots of growth
circles my mounds, hot in the sun,
but my crevices are cool and damp.
Wasps pause, touch their tongues to me.
Jays call and scold.

Dry leaves whisper at me,
nettles thrust up around me
the proof of young boys' piss.
In my very center, a cannabis bush unfurls.
I shift slightly, settle
my bones with the earth's revolutions,
with the pull of the full moon.
Deer bed in the crooks of my elbows,
against the backs of my knees.
And long hairy wasps kiss at my limbs.
Maze jumble, tangle, log jam.
I am light and shadow.

Webs stretch from me.
Cabbage butterflies flutter
whitely through my ribs.
Lichens crawl across my skin.
At night, in the moonlight,
the ruffled edges of my lacy black fungus
shine silver velvet in the moonlight.
Moss and mushrooms.
There are many secret places
and the weeds are taking me back.
Air pushes down from above,
shiny blue flies buzz around me.
Dandelion. Dandelion. Dandelion.

I cannot tell my mushrooms from toadstools.
I am always light and shadow,
thirst and jumble,
full of buzzing, scurrying.
I am food,
I am slowly giving over,
metamorphous,
the sweet smell of sun on grass,
the gentle curve of the earth.
The neighborhood changes often;
I was only poor in spirit at my birth.
I suggest to visitors,
I am more than you ever wanted to know,
the ellipse between old and new forest.
I am slowly giving over,
becoming where instead of what.

Jim Perkinson

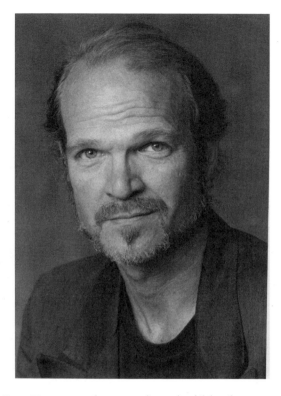

Insoluble Gravity

I first lost my childhood at the age of five to the late afternoon sunlight of July and the huge shadow of a sycamore running the length of the open field behind my house. I was playing cowboys and Indians with friends (I was Roy Rogers, of course!) and suddenly found myself overcome by something hanging softly like eternity in that warm silent air. It was a strange ache in the presence of a strange kind of beauty, as sweet as clover, as overwhelming as memory, as long as the shadow on that field. And I grew instantly old in my five-year-old body, alive for the first time to the mystery of an unutterable sadness inside the innocence of delight.

I next lost it on the basketball court at eight in a rude awakening to another kind of shadow: the mystery of cruelty. It was not a dramatic trauma as traumas go. Just a four-year-long hazing process, clarifying that the world of parochial Catholic boyhood, with all of its little competitions and secrecies, its rituals of acceptance and its language of belonging was superior and closed to the one Protestant kid in that neighborhood who didn't go to the same school. I didn't exactly want to enter that world—it terrified me with its alien-ness. I wanted to make it disappear from the earth. I never quite understood the instinct to turn on the weak that this little neighborhood band seemed to live by. It named me "outcast" before

I even knew what a name could do. I only learned to name it much later. Little ritual celebrations of the "male killer instinct" have confused me ever since.

Which is not to say I didn't become fiercely competitive. I had to, to survive. For against all reason, I quickly developed a passionate love for basketball once I started to play. After a year of only being allowed to throw the ball in from out of bounds (if allowed to play at all), of having the ball wiped off on me if it got muddy (while restrained by two bigger kids), of having muddy shoes wiped off on me (in the same little rite of humiliation), of being constantly shamed about my developing body, and laughed at, and not infrequently beaten and bloodied, I became somewhat adept at the game. In another two years, I had become downright good. I could hold my own, even against bigger opponents.

But physical ability did not translate into social acceptance. I was never included as a friend. After any given game, the court would empty in the direction of one or another of the kids' homes to drink pop and "talk trash." I would suddenly find myself alone with the ball and basket and my frustration against a strange something that seemed to stick to my skin like an invisible disease. I could never see it; but apparently the other kids always did. Over time, I became a stranger even to myself, battling an enemy that I could never quite find.

It all exploded one day on the court, however. A six-foot sixteen-year-old punched me in the stomach while I was still extended after getting off my (twelve-year-old) jump shot against him. The shot went in, but I didn't see it. I was crumpled on the gravel. Four years erupted in screaming tears and flailing fists. I had to jump just to get my hand level with his chest. He knocked me down repeatedly into the crushed stones, until I finally ran home crying. I had barely touched him with my inexperienced swings.

I had, however, (unknowingly) deeply touched my father, who happened to have been watching out of the window in that moment. Unsure how best to respond, not wanting to be overprotective, he and my mom had pretty much left me to deal with the situation alone over those years. He, in particular, had been nursing a fear about me that I would never stand up and fight for myself. Watching that day, he had been tremendously relieved that I had finally struck back, even if I had lost. But I only learned that he had seen me that day years later—too many years later—when the instinct to win acceptance by achievement and competition had all but crushed that young boy's spontaneity. I had indeed learned to be aggressive. But at high cost. It took more than ten years of hard "inner" work to return to the place where I could finally stand eyeball to eyeball with my dad one day and let him look inside and see both pain and love, without trying to deflect his gaze. It took another decade before I could again cry freely.

So often an image has haunted me over the years since— indistinct, not really memory, just a vague "shape." A boy, mute, looking out at a passing world through bars, full of longing, begging with his eyes to be seen and recognized and spoken to. My words now are a tongue-on-loan to that one, offered only so gently, sometimes misleading, sometimes relieving, always only temporary in their ability to construct a home.

But the story is not mine alone. The silent intensity of that four-year initiation into the experience of being outside and somehow strangely "different," without the protection of a father, did not only wound. It birthed knowledge and eventual connection. Adulthood for me has meant an ever-deepening response to yet another "different culture" that I was also early on plunged into. I grew up as a white in a neighborhood in transition and have opted, as an adult, to live continually in inner city neighborhoods largely of color. Slowly, very slowly, I have gained some understanding of a far deeper form of exclusion and a far more violent form of rejection that my own white skin and all of its privileges, wittingly and unwittingly, help perpetrate on those less favored with pink surfaces.

The mute pain within me only very distantly echoes that much more opaque silence our culture has visited on its minorities. But I have found a deep solace in learning constantly from my darker-toned teachers of the "art of overcoming." Today, I find snatches of personal healing only in trying to respond to, and combat, this larger violence I am partially complicit in perpetuating.

I write now because I couldn't speak when it happened to me. But it has not been enough to try to write my own momentary relief.

I have needed a larger communion of groaning. And astonishingly, after a long time of involvement, a whole world of vibrant throbbing release has at times been opened to me despite my whiteness, and coursed through me, and swept me beyond myself, beyond my own little wound, even beyond the bigger wound "my culture" has imposed.

I have found in the world of African-American-inspired urban performance art an entire life-course—indeed, a rich five-hundred-year-old "school"—of using creativity to deflect depravity, of singing when sinking seems imminent, of "slamming" words with such an intensity of life they can momentarily transfigure even death. And I am learning, as I sit at the feet of such vibrant creations, in spite of all the subtle notions of "supremacy" my culture continually whispers in my ear, to learn.

I am learning a word can catch up a body and make it express five meanings at once while the tongue offers but a simple melody line. I am learning "to be spoken"—in "tongues," through my knees, out of my hips and elbows and jerks of the head, through hands dancing counterpoint to lips. I am learning the ecstasy of speaking outside the borderlines of meaning, where meaning is first born as mystery. And I am—gradually! occasionally! briefly!—finding moments of return to an eight-year-old energy that is content to leap without first being certain. Indeed, I even, once in awhile, find again a child before the hot sun, on a late afternoon, caught in wonder.

on trying to heal loss with language

if i try to write away from you
you will create minuscule hollows
between the words into which will
flow, as water on sand,
every scintilla of your cells
until the words themselves
stand quietly hissing your
disappearance
like tidal foam

and if i write towards you
you will submit entirely to each stroke
each period and punctuating
pause, and envelop the thing
with a scent that can't be
smelled, with light that only
comes from the eye and never
enters it, with the sloped nurture
of a single layer of shirt briefly pressed
between your breast last night and
mine this morning
like time without space

and if i just write, ah
then, then i find you
everywhere
like the bone of my hand
like the breath of my lip
like bare flesh
alone
like the memory
that is really the absence
of both of us.

green

is it this?
is it that?

like a taurus in the ice-breath of an aries-dream
awakening to escape and finding dawn is only
more of the same, i refuse
the light . . .

. . . and i still rise looking
for your red tongue on the slick concrete
to lick away the gray
clinging to the tree
standing
like a damp statue
like a statute of little despairs
like the law that says everything must age
and fall down
the buddha points indiscriminate
that or this
is   not
neither is here
now
you are not a brown cry from the ground
not rain from the serengeti
not snow on march peach blossoms, melting
or a tundra mosquito in your legions' legion
creating insanity among the mustangs,
but only the first vein in the first crocus stem appearing
(untended . . . unintended)
beneath my flaking cracked windowsill
and i am your sluggish . . . slow . . . sap
running in the cold heat
of this new spring up your system
without any goal in mind . . . except
the unrelieved hope to become
green   again.

life in flamenco green

what if you lived at the extremity
of your life
like a leaf before wind
drooping heavy in the hot june dark
possessed and naked
in electric blue midnights
running wet with the clean lust of
lightning
when the thunder gods mount
and then whispering and whispering
in the sheets of rain
like a green flamenco dress in
wanton swoonstep to the very edge
of the nothingness over which
you live
lamenting the limitation of stem
and sap and anticipating the one time
you will not be pulled back
to the limb.

hope

it is hard like in rock,
flint shard of a hope
stabbing relentless in the red pulse,
the flesh of a desire to be
home somewhere, anywhere
on the street that has no smell when it is
march cold and wet with the wind,
the letters of the words i spoke to you yesterday
tended like an early garden, soils turned, seeded,
with the proper spacing, waiting in the dark, the damp,
the cold and tremulous,
slowly,
with blind, worm-feeling
movement
the glacial pace
of living hope
buried in backyard soil against the flecks of brick,
shattered bottles, sharp pop-can rings
the doll-headed, tire-blackened, wire-cut dying dirt
of eastside weariness
the ice-pace of hope
in the spring dirt pushing blind
against the blacktop of organized curbside
maintenance, history at the grassroots
where human toes won't go
until their nails stop growing
in somebody else's box
in the dark
below the surface
under my skin and yours
where words are conceived and fight for air
and hope may yet become a bud
on someone's bush
or it may remain a secret lost
and even the worms can't eat
that kind of death.

hearing

what if someone had answered
when you cried the first time?

what if crystal formed when the
next to last tear on the cheek of the
next to last child in the world
dripped onto the street of hunger
and that crystal prism-ed the noon day
demon sun into five arcs of color lighting the
last tear on the last cheek
like a sunset bleeding
around the north pole
into sunrise?

what if your face bent over
that child were in fact always
the possibility of that lighting
as long as you stayed
clear of mirror and led
with your hand
on the bread?

what if that child were
the world's last hope
and its first possibility?

what if you were that child
before you were born into age and anger
before you forgot how to remember
the kiss of taste
the salt of kiss
the god of salt
in a grain of wheat?

could you still sit here
and only listen?

east wall

outside my cob-webbed window
the blue of the winter sky
slowly yellows
heat hissing from the radiator
on the wall, sunlight softens to orange and
with a leap in my chest
i am alone

if someone came to my room
to visit
i would motion to them, shhh
so they would not disturb from its sleep
the luminous dream
of these few fleeting moments

if it sat where i do
even the most hardened heart
would weep
at the slow disappearance
on my east wall.

black and white and spain and tibet

in spain in the 30s
picasso painted
franco's fascist frenzy
as a single plane
reflected in the eye
of an upturned face
vulnerable
fearful
hopeful and hopeless
whose three blue
tears on a
shiny yellow cheek
were also the bombs of that
plane in the
pupil-mirror

in tibet in the 60s
the goddess tara,
emergent millenia ago
(it is said)
from the tear of avalokitesvara
weeping over the world,
breathed her
108 names
in a people
under duress
bleeding over the mountain
passes south
into exile

a bomb on a cheek as a tear
a goddess in a tear as a breath
a people passing south breathing
in pain
in possibility

breathing
in and out
in and out
a people
becoming buddha
becoming tara
becoming paint
on a picasso mandala
the hand and the cheek
the tear and the names
the people over the passes
pain into power
anguish into eloquence
death into life
blue on yellow on red and
your black
and my white
may one day
perhaps
make us
alchemically
whole
if we learn
how to
paint our crying and
cry our naming and
become our breathing
all together
as we flee
over this pass
of now.

dreaming in cracks

eight mile road is the precise
place where america split
in two like a sidewalk crack
of childhood bearing cabalistic doom
and even forty years out from those fears
that line still slices like ontology
step on the crack break your mother's back
step over and cover your own
step on the line and watch your crotch
stay away and pay the fine
double your time, split the lip, scratch the eye, say goodbye
cry the meaning jagged
the story breaks, the fairy shakes, earthquakes
at the heart of a dream of clear and dark
one crack, all cracks
ricocheting splits at the mouth of froth,
the birth of gloom, the glare of noon
on the sidewalk
between eight mile and belle isle
there is crack of dawn full of insoluble gravity
like america sliding into the collapsed hole
of its own unliveable
history.

history in your eye

bottleman over the bridge of lonely
combing belle isle clean of can
bottleman over the street of homely
collecting cup of coke
spit-soaked shard of bent fry
and ketchup-bloodied bun
keeping the sidewalk clear,
you
are the walker over the abyss
it is you who knows the truth
rider of the rail of thought
a slight reflection of night
haunting your sun-shielded eye
a slight reflex-ion of pain
bending your back
reducing shoulder to perpetual hunch
but you know
the truth of things
whose carcasses you handle
like bait
you know the truth of
all such hoards
even though the boardroom
of ford disbelieves
misperceives
does not see you
you know,
and your every
stone cold stare
is a slight sight of america
seen in the mirror of what
it doesn't recognize
and always has been
anyway.

when there is nothing to say

like pepper words whispering
salt in cracks of doom
or quartz-spiked truth
picking god's navel
the poet-mouth spits
teeth razors and arrows
of fornication mingling
taxes with races and
tea with tanks
washing down the boulevard
islanded with poles of information
baptizing all the dancing dramas
of everyday caress
in pubic ciphers of punk
green haircuts sloping
up like newsprint
over the rearview mirror and
this is clearly the mood of brown
laughing down the banal grin
of grimacing gun-holes
in the wall of a thousand sounds
throwing snake eyes across the
bow of every monday
betting it won't drown
and learning it is
already thursday and
the storm was cancelled.
so.
what to say?

god

god is not a mountain you can climb
or an opposition you can sex
god is a grass
root
between toe and ground
full of devouring little mouths
crushed with every least motion you make
crushed in every unthinking step
that shall one day
nonetheless
eat you.

for the birth of sun

light has come
in the night of womb
sheltered its eye
in umbrage
under the belly of mother
light has come
in the quiet of pain
in bloom of youth
under colony
like the power that
makes power possible
like nameless hope
like the strength of suckling breast and
hand on bread kneading
light has come has fallen has stopped
in the dark of deep night
while we sell and buy its glow like a burned leaf
light has wrapped itself in dark
as song of unseen moon
waiting
light has come
light has lit
dark as night
made black the love of white
made love in the tree when the sun is below eye
has made us ground
like loam of hurting help
has come has hid
has wrapped the space of every
inner heart in its soft eye
above the hard lip of freedom
love is the light of the cry
the night of every tiny beating fear
closed in the palm of protection
light, as dark as the only god
i know.

falling

you took the space
between my thumb
and forefinger
and opened it
like a buddha smile
there
not there
not quite there
not quite not there
the wisp
of a hint
of a line
of the lip
in the ghost-appearance
before it advertises
that it will become,
in the next slow-motion eon,
a curled significance
and i fell
into that space
like a night
without stars.

and you were just asking if the next stop was the greyhound station

imperious nose over billboard mouth
nordic scalp-flow of living
alphabet hairs
a samson truth on delilah head
razor eyes over soft syllable teeth
speaking a simple question
speaking question marks like the
space that telescopes time
down to the root of atlantis
and from across the aisle
i boldly ask in turn:
do you know your own name
before you were a lip
over your mama's gum
before you spoke liquid
belches in carniverous rhymes
in a mid-navel rhythm
sea-creature of the dark cave of thought
like a lair of dream?
do you know the meaning of your hip
where the jeans spill south
where belts deceive
where there is no voice?
do you know the lie of truth
that runs every blood red
on the ground of guinea?
do you whisper in
roses?
but out loud, all i say is,
yes.

toeing the line

its proud upturned offering
in the profile of innocent morning
as you stretch in brief articulation
of the groan that defines our
labored impasse—
body begging release
wired like telephone
incessant buzz of question
bee-swarms of anger
exhaustion like a dried riverbed
like the call of wind over granite
like veins of unsmoked coal
like hidden earth—
your lonely breast
yet augurs the ravages
of a month of hot noons
the salt of mouth
the circus of hip
the erection of toe
arched in
wanted agony

and my toe is
once again
reduced to writing
through
my fingers.

amulet hung

the riddle of your cheshire grin
on the limb in the dark
while i, vine-like, clutch bark
hanging half-suspended like some amulet
round your neck, scratching trunk-itch,
searching for substance below that
midnight smile and finding physics
troubled by meaning
the grin an epiphany, a cabalism of the night
unbodied, and what trembles
my hand and fevers twined muscles tense
with climbing suddenly shivers ambiguous
splitting desire into tendrils twisting for a hold
in the beguiled space
looming vacuous under those grinning teeth
the body i grip and the one i seek
suddenly peeling away uncertain like twins
and i, caught dangling
suspended between eye and hand
reading double in the dark
secreted into the dream-edges that color
all realities and even less thralled encounters
left solemn and
thrashing in the soft tides
of your sleeping breath, but tremored
and touched
and scratching now, gentle and fond,
the twilight of your lingering absence
from the tip of my pen.

iridescence

in every line of color shimmers
iridescent
a distant drum throb
the sadness of bougainvillea
hanging pink over wrought iron

every brush-stroke of hair out of place
summons invisible powers
from floorboards
out of sinks
below ground

each precisely pronounced sentence shivers
momentarily on the tongue in
another voice like
liquid transcendence
inhabiting a coke bottle
on that rickety table
in the back yard

and leaves swirl
and skirts swirl
and flowers fall
and night falls
and feet beat
the damp earth, the dust
into home of spirit
and tears fall
and laughter lingers on the air like
charcoal fire smoke in the dark
curling around chicken meat
and the hand claps
and the drum beats
and the heart throbs
and the blood runs
and the mind blazes with unknown thoughts

dreaming words
dreaming saliva
and nietzsche was almost right:
god is the death
of all grammar, or rather
grammar is the death
of all the gods of frenzy and hope
but this is not order
this body
of every fallen tree
talking under the water
on the side of the mountain
where it came from
this indigo etching
on the nothing of white bark
pretending to truth

this is just another poem
to the grief of every
miscarried idea of beauty
every fallen leaf
every least dead mosquito
every one of us flickering now
before we become
a pressed flower
in someone else's notebook
we are all color
before the midnight star
we are all the waters of an ancient ocean
that cries no more against the sand
we are mere spray   hanging
briefly
iridescent
before the single flash of sun
that is our only and greatest
significance.

About the Writers

Margo LaGattuta, editor, is a poet with four books: *Embracing the Fall* (Plain View Press), *The Dream Givers* (Lake Shore Publishing), *Noedgelines* (Earhart Press) and *Diversion Road* (State Street Press). This is the fifth Michigan anthology she has edited for Plain View Press. The others are: *Variations on the Ordinary, Almost Touching, Up from the Soles of Our Feet,* and *At the Edge of Mirror Lake*. She co-edited and has poetry appearing in *Wind Eyes* and *Everywhere is Someplace Else*. Her book of essays, *The Heart Before the Course*, will be released this year. She has an MFA in writing from Vermont College, teaches writing at Oakland Community College and University of Michigan-Flint and hosts a weekly radio program. She is associate editor and columnist for *Surburban Lifestyles* newspaper and writes a column for *Phenomenews*.

R. Suzanne Zeitman planned to change her undergraduate major to English but instead finished with a BA in mathematics in 1970. Subsequent degrees, resulting from two separate returns to school, are in mathematics and computer science, the last of these a PhD completed in 1994. Suzanne is employed as an associate editor of *Mathematical Reviews* and loves her job, in part because it requires skill in both mathematics and language. She began writing poetry in 1997 while attending a workshop at a local library. Though having suspected all along that she would eventually start writing, she remains amazed at how complicated and inevitable *eventually* can be. Suzanne lives with her husband, Jerry Grossman, in Rochester Hills, Michigan. Their daughter, Pamela, was killed by a motorist in 1990 at the age of six.

Tamara Graham is a storyteller. She carries on in the oral and written traditions of her north Georgia and east Tennessee roots. She never had any intention of speaking or writing beyond her own four walls until her good friend, Bob Shaw, convinced her that she could, and should, create something besides training proposals. She dedicates her work to her most amazing family but most especially to Essie Nevada Beckler Ogletree, her own special Grandmama.

Ann Holdreith has a degree in Fine Art from the University of Detroit. She taught art for sixteen years in the Royal Oak Public Schools and her paintings have been displayed by several Michigan galleries. For the past thirteen years, she has focused on the Performing Arts. She is a trained vocalist and actress, works on stage and in film, and is lead vocalist in an experimental music band. She integrates these performance skills with her poetry and has been featured as a performance poet at several Detroit venues, including the Michigan Opera Theatre and Wayne State University. Ann has presented her improvisation classes, which combine theatre, movement and spirituality, since 1987, and she presents innovation training to Fortune 500 companies. She teaches for the Detroit Writer's Voice, is published by Gravity Press and is included in an anthology of Detroit poets from Wayne State University. Her work is dedicated to the full expression of the human spirit.

John Morris has had careers as a conventional minister, a professional philosopher, and a computer specialist. He holds an MDiv degree in counseling from Starr King School in Berkeley and a PhD in philosophy from Michigan State University. He currently works as a volunteer with several alternative religious groups. The constant factor through all these lives has been his writing, primarily in the form of several hundred articles for various journals and reports. He lives in Ann Arbor, where he helps to edit a monthly newsletter, *The Seeker Journal,* and co-lead classes in Hearth Witchery.

Joyce Harlukowicz has spent the last twenty-four years in large rooms with noisy children, teaching elementary, middle school, and high school physical education. She intends to spend the next twenty-four years in small rooms with noisy children teaching middle school language arts for the Imlay City Community Schools. Her love of writing was nurtured early by the gifted English teacher Michael Marsee and others in the Troy Public Schools. She has published numerous training handbooks, articles in professional journals, and education research.Joyce has an undergraduate degree from Central Michigan University and a master's degree in Educational Administration from Michigan State University. She is a resident of Rochester Hills, Michigan.

Patricia Washburn has a BA in psychology from Oakland University. Besides poems and stories for her children, she's written travel pieces, human interest articles, short fiction, and creative non-fiction. Her work has appeared in various publications including *The Eccentric* and *The Detroit Free Press*. She grew up on the north side of Chicago in a neighborhood known as Rogers Park. At age twenty, she married her high school sweetheart, Robert. They have four grown children (two daughters and two sons), a steadily increasing number of grandchildren, and a dog named Logan.

Dale Prentiss enjoyed only two high school classes: Philosophy of Man and Nature and Creative Writing. What a combination: creativity, philosophy, nature, and interesting teachers. But then he went on to get three degrees in the less creative, indoor-only discipline of US history, earning a BA from the University of Michigan and an MA and PhD from Stanford University. In 1989, he traveled to Sweden under a Fulbright Fellowship (researching emigration and the "American melting pot" theory), taught history the next year at Oakland University, and began in 1991 to work full-time as a historian for the federal government. That job involved writing, editing, program managing, publishing, and even documentary film-making. But only after Dale left that job in April 1999 could he once again combine creative writing, philosophy, nature, and interesting teachers. He is now a writer, consultant, and the founder and producer of Ironwork Retreats (ironworkretreats.com).

Rhonda Hacker is a carpenter, cabinetmaker, and caregiver. These days she works as a letter carrier and at finding her voice as a writer. Some of her stories come out of work experience, but her real mainstay is family and friends. They've given her not only subject matter, but the encouragement to write in the first place and to persevere when the going gets tough.

If she hadn't flunked college chemistry on her way to an anticipated career as a research biologist, **Linda Dominik** would not have gotten a BA in English Literature from Nazareth College in Rochester, New York. Following graduation from Unity Ministerial School in

Kansas City, she served as minister in Syracuse and Cincinnati and currently leads a congregation at Unity-North Church in Orion Township, Michigan, where she is Senior Minister. She has written for numerous church publications and considers herself primarily a prose writer. A Troy resident, she lives with her wonderdog, PK.

Maureen Dunphy received her BA in English at Oakland University and, after doing post-graduate work at Wayne State University in English and sixteen years as a writer in the field of training and communications, her MFA from Goddard College in Plainfield, Vermont. She teaches fiction-writing at Oakland University and composition and creative writing at Oakland Community College, Orchard Ridge. She has been published in the on-line *Ironwork Journal* (ironworkretreats.com) and has a piece, "Getting There from Here," coming out in *Peninsula*, an anthology of creative non-fiction to be published by Michigan State University Press. She is a facilitator of writing workshops, retreats, and conferences and the producer of "All the Write Stuff," a series of creative writing workshops for young writers. She resides in "Fashionable Ferndale" with her husband, two daughters, four cats, one rabbit and a Siamese fighting fish named Leopold.

Jim Perkinson is a longtime resident of inner city Detroit, currently teaching courses on world religions, racism, death and dying, and social ethics at a number of area colleges (Marygrove College, University of Detroit, Central Michigan University, Ecumenical Theological Seminary). After years as part of an activist urban religious community comprised of both married and single people, organizing housing development projects on the near east-side, Jim got his PhD at the University of Chicago in theology/history of religions. He now focuses his writing, both academic and creative, on experiences where politics and spirituality intersect. Both urban intensity and natural beauty are integral to his sense of meaning and his poetics of representation.